Praise for
Black Female Interracial and Intercultural Marriage Book 1: First and Foremost
From Amazon Review Page

"**A Must Read for Every Black Woman!** The author of this book, for the past three years has been a steadfast positive influence for Black women everywhere…She advocates living well without making apologies! Sadly, many believe that Black women should accept a "lowly" or "servants" stance in life…Not so…This writing is a comprehensive guide to why it is essential for Black women to select quality mates from the get-go…I urge the reader to purchase this book and pass it along to other women in their circle…I also recommend this to the younger Black woman who is beginning to take an interest in the opposite sex, as it will give advance preparation…Eagerly awaiting the second book!"

~~**Cher, BlackWomenDeserveBetter.com**

"**First and Foremost**" is a terrific, practical book and guide for black women young and old alike. Ms. Moore shares her profound and common-sense perspectives on black woman and white male marriage and relationships. It is not difficult to understand why the author's popularity soared as more and more black women were drawn into the fact-packed essays and discussions as it seems that you are watching the dialogue take place.

I appreciate Ms. Moore's genuine concern (not condescension) for black women as we realize the boundaries that have been overtly and covertly placed on us within the black community. Those discarding the bill of goods will come away intrigued, determined and knowing they can do better and get better. This book is vital to understanding why we should be seeking a quality mate and living well. Readers will look forward to next book in this exciting series!"

~~**Swirl Queen**

"I'm a young black woman who just started dating so this book really laid to rest any doubts I had about interracial dating and marriage. Usually, when I was with family or watching black shows (comedy or drama) someone always has to make a loud declaration about how "black women aren't attracted to white men" or how the white man will always hate the black man. Admittedly, I've always been attracted to black men as well as men of other races but I just absorbed the messages that men of other races would find me unattractive and that I shouldn't even bother being attracted to them. Of course, it began to dawn on me, through experience, that what seemed like common sense at the time was incredibly stupid. I began to discover that I attracted a lot black men but they disrespectful towards me and my creep detector went off more than once. The black men I developed crushes on were friendly, clever, witty and we shared the same interests but I would always discover that they exclusively dated women of other races (some would even tell me why they disliked black women since we're such good friends and I'm not like "those" black women lol!).

Well meanwhile, I'd been approached by white men who were sweet and respectful but by golly I was just too anxious about the idea of dating outside my race! The whole thing seems really ridiculous now. Well, its 2012, I just turned 24 and with the help of Eve's blog and book I'm seriously over the race thing. Until Evia's blog and book, I didn't know that a large majority of people in the world did not live in fear, paranoia, loneliness, and worn out ideas because they simply refused to. They moved on and I knew I wanted to be one of them so…I moved on too, haha. This book also tackles a lot of sticky topics like *race loyalty, stereotypes, colorism, class and education* within America and the black community.

Evia and other bloggers like her are so intelligent and wise, that I can honestly say I learned a lot more from this book (and her blog) than I ever did in sociology class! I'm gonna definitely check out her other books in the future. A lot of people give lip service to the notion of colorblindness nowadays but their actions say otherwise: don't be one of those people! Challenge yourself and dare to be authentic. Reading this book is a good way to start."

~~**Daisy**

Also by **Eve Sharon Moore**

More titles in the series in paperback and for e-readers:

CHOICES: Black Women Interracial and Intercultural Marriage—BOOK 2

RECIPROCITY: Black Women Interracial and Intercultural Marriage—BOOK 3

LIVING WELL: Black Women Interracial and Intercultural Marriage—BOOK 4

Black Women: Interracial and Intercultural Marriage
Book 1—First and Foremost

SECOND EDITION

—Conversations on Black Women Making Commonsense Choices, Marrying, and Living Well—

Eve Sharon Moore

SHAREVE COMMUNICATIONS
A Division of Southern Girls General Store, Inc.

Black Women Interracial and Intercultural Marriage: BOOK 1–First and Foremost, 2nd Edition

Copyright © 2012 by Eve Sharon Moore

ISBN 978-1-937587-00-0

Published in the United States of America by Shareve Communications, a Division *of Southern Girls General Store, Inc.*, 1390 Columbia Ave., #215, Lancaster, PA 17603, USA

Digital 2nd edition of this book published 2012 by Shareve Communications

Paperback 1st Edition © 2009 published by Createspace Books

Digital 1st edition © 2009 by Shareve Communications

All rights reserved. No part of this book may be reproduced in any form or by any electronic or mechanical means including information storage and retrieval systems without permission in writing from the publisher.

Printed in the United States of America

To:

my awesome sons: my greatest reward for living,

my visionary grandmother who instilled in me the common sense to stay on the path, and

my loving mates who shared their wisdom and supported me in all of my endeavors.

Choosing a mate is the single most important decision that a woman makes in her life, especially if there are to be children. If she chooses her mate wisely, she and her children will reap many rewards. But if she chooses poorly, she has paved the way for herself and her offspring to suffer, for generations!

—Eve Sharon Moore

CONTENTS

	Introduction	15
1	Nothing Pathological About It	29
2	A Good Mate Can Be Any Skin Shade	35
3	Don't Hate Me Because I Married a Good Man	39
4	The Mating War	45
5	Why Do People Ask Us How We Met?	53
6	Black Women—NEVER Accept Scraps!	57
7	Anger is for Losers	69
8	The Loving Case—40th Anniversary	83
9	Do White Men "Step Up" To Black Women?	89
10	Prison Inmate Lovers	113
11	Sabotage Again—Do Black Women Push White Men Away?	127
12	Alec Wek, Black Women's Beauty, and White Men	133
	Glossary	197

INTRODUCTION

THE ORIGIN OF THIS BOOK:

Black Women Interracial and Intercultural Marriage BOOK 1—First and Foremost is the first book in the ongoing series, compiling my commonsense essays and conversations with thousands of readers regarding the surge in black women—mainly upwardly mobile African-American in the United States—choosing to mingle romantically with and marry men from other races and cultures. This is also known as *out-marriage* and *exogamy*. Some people consider this turn of events revolutionary and evolutionary in the social sense for black women because the overwhelming majority of these non-black men who date and marry black women are white men.

In the past, virtually 100% of African-American women married only African-American men or black men. However, two conditions have drastically changed this pattern: (1) greatly lessened racial and social barriers between white men and upwardly-mobile black women in the United States, and (2) a large percentage of African-American men do not seek marriage, or are either not available or not prepared for marriage, for a variety of reasons.

Approximately 35% of African-American men are married, presently. Twenty-two percent of them married non-black women in

2008. Among African-American women, about 70% are presently unmarried.

When conditions in the environment change negatively, people with common sense, who plan to survive and thrive, also change their behavior to offset these unfavorable conditions. African American women out-marrying men of other races and cultures is the normal or commonsense response, given these markedly altered social conditions.

I am an African-American woman, a writer, and a lifelong student of comparative cultures or *ethnology,* my undergraduate major. My first marriage was to a born-and-bred West African man with whom I shared a multi-year marriage and many enlightening experiences regarding culture and race while living both in Africa and the United States with him. I'm now married to an American white man.

My series of books will serve the future as a record of much in the hearts and minds of black women currently as well as the views of a cross-section of others regarding the prevailing circumstances that surround black women out-marrying, in the first decades of this millennium. Capturing Black women's views as events unfold about the circumstances in their lives is of significant historical importance. Future readers will read exactly what black women were thinking during this time, and in their own words about various factors in their lives.

Historical accounts about the lives of black people are usually devoid of black women's perspectives, or only have a sparse representation. The series of essays in each of my books and the broad scope of the accompanying thousands of comments in the entire series will thus help to fill that critical void.

Many black women, men of various races, and others are avid readers and viewers of my site. In the numerous notes I've received, they have hailed the value of both my commonsense perspectives as well as the views and experiences of many of the commenters. They love and learn from the conversations.

On my website, I share my thoughts and a wide variety of experiences from my decades-long journal, recounting my life as an interculturally and interracially married woman. I often advise my readers to "take what you can use and toss the rest." I'm known on my website as "Evia."

Introduction

As a strong proponent of quality relationships and marriages for African-American women, the gist of many of my essays urges black women in the United States, in particular, to broaden their dating and marriage scope to include quality men from the entire global village. I implore them to take a proactive stand on this issue of finding a suitable and compatible, quality mate of any race or ethnic background. The quality of the man is the most important factor. Black women must vet each suitor and look for evidence that he possesses the traits, abilities, desire, and drive to meet the challenges of performing well as a husband and a father. The world is now a global village. African-American women who seek marriage and children must rip themselves from their comfort zone, when necessary, and mingle fluidly in the world, but only with compatible men who possess the capabilities that indicate a high likelihood of strong performance as husbands and fathers.

A great proportion of African-American women seek to find a loving and lovable mate of quality, marry, and have children—in that order. Therefore, the central theme of my essays is to encourage African-American women to realize that they have many choices available towards reaching that goal.

I stress that black women must choose mates wisely. They must be radically proactive regarding mating only with quality, loving, lovable, suitable, and compatible men. The core purpose of my essays is to energize and activate African-American women towards that end. I urge them to reach out and embrace the many choices beyond their immediate environment for a fulfilling life, including love and marriage to a quality mate.

I define a quality man, in this regard, as one who is ready, willing, and capable emotionally, mentally, and financially of meeting the challenges of life as an adult male. Or, if he's a younger man, he must be in serious preparation to do so.

The essence of creating a quality life is another theme I've written much on in some of my essays. I compel African-American women to live an abundant life in all respects, or to "live well." For many women, a loving, committed mate is an important component in living a life of abundance.

In July 2006, when I began writing these hundreds of blog essays that make up my continuing series of what I consider now "teaching" essays, I was a newbie blogger. I naively had no clue that anyone would be particularly interested in reading what I wrote about my marriage to a white man. My blog was my journal—not a private one, but a written account of some of my experiences as an interracially married woman.

I had dated men of other nationalities and races since I was eighteen. Since I majored in ethnology as an undergraduate in college, I wrote often about intercultural relationships. I married a Nigerian man, and lived in Nigeria with him. The dynamics of intercultural and interracial relationships were the norm for me. Therefore, my decision to marry a white man was not an unusual move for me.

I soon discovered I had encountered a virtual 'live wire' by openly discussing a topic in my essays that many people consider taboo. My happy marriage to a white man was just more than many people could stomach in 2006. Although I received an overwhelming number of supportive notes in my e-mailbox, it also became obvious that my essays irritated some, to the extent that they wished a monstrous caterpillar would swallow me.

Please note that African-Americans are the "black" reference group for my essays, although there may be similar concerns among other groups of blacks. Many black people in the United States still have great difficulty discussing the topic of black women and white men dating or black women entering loving, marital relationships with white men, or anything regarding interracial relationships of the black woman-white-skinned man type. A number of researchers have contacted me saying it's difficult to find material at all about the black woman-white man relationship, unless it's sexual or pornographic, despite the surge in black woman-white man dating and marriages.

People are simply not talking or writing about it, or only scantily. Many are apparently very reluctant to discuss this topic because of the ever-strained state of race relations in the United States, which is due to present-day racist structures stemming from the country's sordid history of chattel slavery perpetrated upon captured Africans by Europeans.

However, if there were courses on interracial dating, love, sex, and marriage between black women and white, or Euro-American men, around the turn of the millennium in the United States, this series of essays, particularly the thousands of penetrating comments from a cross-section of readers, would be required reading. In a nutshell, the comments from my readers are powerful. They literally changed the course of my life.

All the essays and comments in my books are plucked from my blog site: BlackFemale Interracial Marriage Ezine, located now at **www.blackfemaleinterracialmarriage.com**, which my readers have made enormously popular by visiting to the tune of millions of visits since July 2006. They've read millions of words of my writings, along with the numerous comments from readers. I thank them for spreading my name throughout the blogosphere and bringing many other readers to my site, many of whom have written me to say that my essays have uplifted them and spurred them to make life-altering changes.

From the very beginning, I was contacted for interviews by academicians, other bloggers, magazines, newspapers, radio and TV program producers, and in early 2007, I was contacted by a reporter from the Associated Press, who did a series of interviews with me for an article regarding black women in interracial relationships and marriages with white men. This culminated in an August 2007 Associated Press article on the subject, and my blog was spotlighted. The article was picked up by CNN online news, USA Today, ABC news and numerous major and minor news outlets worldwide and went viral.

Within 36 hours of the article appearing, more than 10,000 visitors came to my site from all parts of the globe. I was amazed that a topic as familiar to me as sliced bread could interest so many people!

Others often describe me as "courageous." I've never thought of myself as that. I am, however, a strong proponent of marriage for African-American women. I'm a believer in practical consequences and real effects, a pragmatist. Many among the 70% of black women in the United States are unmarried largely due to the unavailability of quality marriage mates in the pool of men they've been traditionally slated to marry—black American men. Therefore, it is merely logical for these women to broaden their dating and marriage pool to include *all* interested, suitable, and compatible men of quality in the global village. As you read some of the thousands of comments that accompany the whole series of essays, it becomes apparent that the overwhelming majority of upwardly mobile African-American women commenters agree with this sheer commonsense remedy.

In the United States, the bulk of the non-black men are white American men. Whites or white-skinned people comprise roughly 70% (2006 Census) of the U.S. population, and blacks are 13%. Many African-American women share a familiar set of values and cultural background with many white American men.

In 2009, however, my commonsense position is largely considered radical and even heretical in segments of the black community in the United States, even though most blacks know that the pool of marriageable black men and those who are interested in marriage have shrunk to a thin stream. Seemingly, many black people would prefer that these black women remain unmarried. At the same time, black women in America are constantly criticized for having children out of wedlock—the "babymama" phenomenon.

The women obviously cannot marry unavailable black men or those who lack interest, and they shouldn't marry unloving men, or those who are unequipped to meet the challenges of marriage and family life. However, no high profile black "leader," black politician, thought leader, or anyone of national visibility has addressed the issue of *who* these millions of women are supposed to marry *before* having children.

Despite that, even the mere suggestion that it would make good sense for black women to include white men in their pool of committed relationship candidates is met with anger, accusations of "disloyalty to black men," "sellout," and sometimes—physical threats by black men, some of whom exclusively date and marry interracially themselves. Many black men express their approval of blacks interracially dating and marrying—but for black men only.

The volumes of fear and confusion expressed by the black women commenters regarding IR dating and marriage fascinated me. Their sentiments were unfamiliar to me, since I have always dated and married outside my group. Their feelings became a major incentive to continue writing the essays. Fearful of black community condemnation and ostracism, many so-called "strong" black women succumb to community and self-inflicted pressure to mate with the only "approved" man—a black man, at a time when there is a critical shortage of marriageable and marriage-interested American black men.

This often results in man sharing or serially mating with black men who have not equipped themselves to meet the emotional and financial responsibilities of a relationship with a woman or the demands of fatherhood. Numerous other black women simply wed themselves to the church or community and live a life of solitary confinement on the romantic front as they wait in quiet desperation for their "Mr. Right Black Man" to appear.

Although some people tend to view African-American women as amazingly strong, which is translated as something akin to a separate species of mythical Amazonian women, I want to emphasize that African-American women are the same as other women around the world. They dream of children and a stable home life with a responsible, supportive, loving partner at their side. Given that so few of them are able to readily attain this, many of them are frequently encouraged by other blacks in their social circle to wait endlessly for their 'black knight' to appear.

In order to keep the women complacent while waiting, this ever-adapting message continues to contort itself to explain to the women why he hasn't appeared, yet. To remain hopeful inside their comfort zone, which is usually within black community circles, many of the women cooperate in helping to delude other black women to remain patient and waiting too. A proportion of them put on a brave face each day and takes refuge in what I've labeled in this context as *magical thinking*.

Many non-African-Americans, including other black ethnics, are not aware of this highly effective indoctrination process that maintains the status quo inside the African-American community. Some of these others have asked me why it is that so many hard-working, seemingly intelligent black women limit themselves to African-American men as mates and focus, usually without help from the fathers, on raising the children and 'saving the black community,' yet receive merely minimal gratitude, if any, for their sacrifices and effort.

Despite the devastating toll it takes on their emotional and physical health, along with their finances, the fact is that often, many of the women themselves can't explain in any rational way why they do it. There is certainly no logical reason to continue investing the bulk of assets (time, energy, money, life focus) in any entity that continues to deliver faint or negative returns. Many African-American women remain stoically on this course, however, and continue to end up struggling, poor, and alone.

As many of the comments clearly state or reveal, this is very harmful to the women and this is evident in the dismal health statistics of black women, many of whom "medicate" themselves in various ways. One apparent way is with food, and they lead the nation in 2009 in weight-related illnesses: diabetes, cancer, heart problems, and a host of other debilitating maladies. Commenters continually make the point that the black community could not survive without 'riding on the backs' of black women, yet does not consider it important to make the basic needs of black women, a priority. Aside from lip service, there is nothing in the situation that even shows there is a functioning "community" involved. A community is a give-and-take place. There is a large degree of uplifting, mutual exchange, or reciprocity between people who live in a functioning, actual *community*.

The conclusion from dozens of discussions and hundreds of comments is: Reciprocity is sorely lacking in the so-called *black community*, when it comes to meeting the basic needs of African-American women. Many of the black men, who had the resources to help, have fled physically, mentally, and emotionally.

Therefore, from the standpoint of many blacks who remain in a black residential area and even those who inhabit mainly a "black" mental construct, but who may live outside of the physical black residential area, this deluding of black women will continue—in order for the women to maintain the *illusion* of the black "community."

Many black women therefore receive much subtle pressure from black men and from other black women to believe in and keep in place a safe harbor for everyone but themselves. Indoctrinated to put their own safety, security, and general betterment low on the list, many African-American women are strongly complicit in supporting an arrangement that does not meet their needs or those of other American black women.

Reciprocity is critical in any healthy or worthwhile relationship. High praise is often given to black women who give selflessly to the community, but most of the women have not learned to demand that others meet their needs, or give back to them.

Shortly after I began blogging, many black women came to my site to discuss their frustrations about being boxed in by the so-called 'black community.' Woman after woman pointed out that the "community:" 1) provides no effective protection from the misogyny nor the general violence and sexual attacks from an assortment of community predators who physically and emotionally prey on women and children, often with impunity, 2) presents severely low-quality, limited, or nonexistent marital options, 3) often blames the women for the community's demise, 4) burdens them (like 'mules') alone with the task of "saving the community," 5) expects black women to successfully socialize and raise male children alone, a feat that is unparalleled in general human history, 6) pressures black women to prop up or carry severely dysfunctional or damaged beyond repair black males (Dbrbm), 7) offers scant or no reciprocity to black women for the sacrifices made by them to keep the traditional black church and black community from disappearing altogether.

Much of the women's discontent also focuses on the unabashed double standard—held by many American black men and some segments of black women—that gives tacit approval for black men to date, love, and marry non-black women while pressuring black women to remain "loyal" to black men only.

My blog became the site of a rallying cry from a wide cross-section of black women with the central message that black women must make use of their options to meet and marry mates from the entire global village just as black men increasingly do and just as white, Asian, Hispanic, and other women and men do. Black women in America cannot mend or hold up the black community, alone. Instead, black men are needed to build, repair, and sustain the community with equal involvement and commitment. Without that, the American black community will continue to sink.

Some of my readers and I encouraged others to spread the commonsense remedy that African-American and other black women in a similar predicament must exercise all of their options to mingle with and marry the highest quality, compatible, loving, and lovable man of any skin shade or background. They must do this from their early adult years. Since the vast majority of the women feels that they lack a community that protects them and safeguards their interests, black women must make it a priority to promote and protect their own interests, 'first and foremost.' Each woman lifting herself will lift the entire community.

I urged readers to start their own blogs to help to get the word to millions of black women that no woman is alone in her yearnings for a loving partner and fulfillment as a woman. My essays and the poignant comments struck a chord with many black women in the United States and beyond who endure sexist oppression that compounds the racial oppression many black women face. They heard the word and responded.

Thus, my blog and similar ones that sprang up became "freedom" oases offering understanding, acceptance, support, encouragement, ideas, strategies, tactics, and practical advice for numerous black women who visited often to mingle with like-minded others. They, in essence, have formed the community they've been looking for. These women sought affirmation and guidance from a caring sisterhood as they strove to actualize their goal of finding loving and lovable, quality men for partners, and securing a relationship with fully committed men who possess fatherhood desires and the emotional and financial ability to be involved fathers in the lives of their children. Millions of black women in the U.S. desire marriage before having children, and want, in general, to exercise their options to 'live well.' These are normal desires of most women worldwide. African-American women are no different.

However, when typical African-American women express these desires, they do not often get the support of other blacks around them. Those around them frequently scold them for being impatient and "selfish." They are told to focus primarily on uplifting the black community, first. Others, who they trust, urge them to subscribe to the notion that their "Mr. Right" is on the way. Confused and lacking support, many black women give in to this social pressure. They neglect their own needs. They wait or they settle for an unsuitable male.

Through my essays and the comments section, many of the women began to realize that they must not limit themselves in any way. Marriage-oriented African-American women must not waste time with a focus on any man who is not interested in a committed relationship or marriage.

One of my more controversial positions is my frequent urgings to black women to "marry well," by marrying a man who is at least as equally upwardly-mobile and ambitious as the woman is. I explain, in meticulous detail, why any woman of childbearing age has to be extremely particular in choosing the man she spends time with sexually, in order to avoid abortions, unplanned children, and blighted lives.

Introduction

In 2009, single black women with children comprise the most impoverished demographic in the country. My mantra is: *The choice of a sexual mate is the single most important decision a woman makes in her life since its impact will more than likely be felt for generations. Based on her choice, she—and any child who may come from this sexual intimacy—will sink or soar.*

Detractors deliberately misinterpret me when I urge black women to include progressive-minded, enlightened white men and other non-black men in their dating and marriage pool. This is often distorted to mean that I am telling black women to embrace racist white men and reject all black men. This amounts to outright lies and gross twisting of my message, since I have never encouraged any association between black women and racist men or the rejection of quality black men. These contrived distortions aim to discredit my message and cause fear.

Most black women readers shrewdly saw through these attempts to discredit me and my message. They stated in private notes to me and in their comments that the major underlying purpose of the critics' lies is—to keep as many black women as possible, confused and available as a "safety net" for favors and as sexual partners for black men to use as they wish. This is often why even black men who exclusively date or are married to non-black women, still don't want black women to date or marry white men.

A black male commenter stated that some African-American men also have the fear that as more black women date and marry non-black men and non-African American men, the desirability index of AA men as sexual and relationship partners will be reduced among women, generally. He said some AA men reason that high demand for them pushes up their value in the mating market among *all* women.

The critical point that my essays and the comments focus on throughout this maze of emotions, perspectives, and politics is the lack of regard for black women's needs as individual women—the right of each black woman to 'live well.' What quickly becomes apparent is that the black woman's right to opportunities for love and happiness is rarely seen as a priority by anyone, not even by the women themselves.

Both the positive and negative responses to my blog became so overwhelmingly intense at times that I had to take breaks from it frequently. Being on the forefront of what some have called a "black women's empowerment" movement (though I consider it to be the common sense imperative) is emotionally draining. Many people feel they have the right to dictate to an American black woman how she should think, how she should live her life, who she should love or shouldn't love, or whether she should even be loved. I frequently remind black women that the Constitution of the United States grants every adult the right to choose the person of their choice to love and marry, irrespective of race, culture, religion, etc.

My essays compel black women to look out for their interests 'first and foremost' (subtitle of this book) and without apology. This is common sense because 'self-preservation is the first law of nature.' Black women must make it a priority to prepare and position themselves early in life to, not only survive, but also *thrive*. They will succeed at doing this only if they make it a rule to promote and protect their interests and require reciprocity from others.

The primary lesson that I want women readers to draw from my blog's teaching essays regarding love and marriage is that a "good lovin" man can be from any compatible background, and of any skin shade or race. African-American women of marriageable age should focus on marriage to a quality man as the goal, especially if the woman plans to have children. Though marriage is not a perfect institution, it's the best arrangement that humans have devised for having and rearing children and for meeting myriad other needs of women and men.

A family starts with marriage—a legal commitment or one that is sanctioned by a particular culture or society. It is the basic building block of any community or nation. When the majority in any community consists of non-committed men and women engaging in recreational, no-strings-attached sex with each other, the result will always be social chaos, as we currently see in many black residential areas. For this reason, there won't be any significant improvement in the American black community until a large percentage of the residents begin choosing mates properly, and marrying with the focus on a family bond. There is no way around this.

This is why I stress that black women in the West who seek quality mates for marriage must broaden their selection pool by including men from all backgrounds. As I frequently point out, "there are many more men of quality in the ocean than in a backyard puddle." It is the common sense imperative for American black women, in particular, to embrace the wide variety of men in the global village who appreciate their beauty and worth, men who regard them as desirable mates for marriage, and to become indifferent towards any man who views them otherwise.

American black women who desire marriage must promote the message that they desire marriage, but only with men who are equipped for, or (depending on age) can show evidence that they are equipping themselves for marriage (emotionally and financially). It is foolish for a black woman who wants to marry to spend time with any man who does not meet these simple criteria.

It would seem unnecessary, but I want to emphasize to upwardly mobile American black women that there is no shortage of quality men in the global village. The women simply must enlarge their selection pool. There are numerous black ethnic men (intercultural option), white men, white-skinned men (interracial option), and other men in America and throughout the world who are very much attracted to black women's beauty, sense of purpose, and being. I hear from many of these men. Yet, too often, both sides tend to focus excessively on race and other minor, surface details.

My husband and I both realize that "race" is simply a social construction, created and kept alive by immoral, self-centered, human beings who have exploited the worst in human nature to keep a lot of "white" and "black" people stuck inside the race construct, while selected others reap the benefits and privileges. My husband's skin shade is lighter than mine is, and my hair, with its much tighter coil, differs from his by the degree of the coil. All the rest is simply a part of the "race" fairy tale or nightmare.

There is no essential difference between "races" of human beings. Progressive-minded, thriving-oriented people realize they are being manipulated and do not cooperate with the construction of race.

[NOTE 1: www.blackfemaleinterracialmarriage.com is the Ezine companion to this book. Most pictures cited in this book, plus numerous other photos of famous and ordinary interracial or intercultural couples comprised of black women and their non-black or other-culture spouses or significant others, can be viewed in picture galleries at the Ezine or accessed there. While at the site, please browse through the sections containing a wide array of videos, articles, links, and podcasts related to this topic.

NOTE 2: Most of the teaching essays and the accompanying comments are or will be available for purchase in various formats: paperback, audio, and for a variety of e-reading devices.

NOTE 3: Most of the essays in this book are out of the sequence in which they were written. The comments from readers are presented—as received, except for editing of gross misspellings, typos, and grammar styles that would interfere with reader comprehension. (Some commenters are non-Americans, which is reflected in the spellings of certain words.) All comments were supplied voluntarily and with the knowledge they would be published.

Abbreviations, colloquialisms, and vernacular expressions are explained in the Glossary. I welcome your comments, questions, suggestions, and helpful corrections. Please share them with me at: **eviamoore@gmail.com**]

1

Nothing Pathological About It

July 4, 2006, 9:43 a.m.

A few days ago, I got the idea to create my own blog about my interracial marriage to a white man after reading the blog of a black British woman, Halima Sal-Anderson, who has also written a book about interracial relationships involving black women and white men. In her book, Halima urges upwardly mobile black women to examine the issue of interracial relationships more closely, considering the shrinking pool of similarly situated black men who seek marriage.

I had thought about writing something—a book, even—about my relationship before but never went through with it. I now feel more compelled to write, especially after reading so many *warped* views from blacks and others about what they "think" motivates blacks to cross racial lines in the "race" construct for what's commonly known as an "interracial relationship" or IR.

I certainly don't believe *all* black and white people marry into other races for the *right* or emotionally healthy reasons, but I want to go on record by saying I married my husband, Darren, simply because of our loving feelings for each other and because I believed he would be a good mate to me in every way I wished a mate to be. I did not marry him for "social acceptance" or because of "self-hate" or because I wanted to "lighten my babies" or for "his money" or for any of the other twisted notions some people obviously project onto me when they see me with him. These are *their* issues, not mine.

I was simply a woman who wanted to re-marry and he–a man of quality—came into my life and treated me in a loving manner, and asked me to marry him. If a loving and lovable, quality black man or any other man had come along and treated me in a similar manner, it's very likely I would have married him. It's just that simple, folks. Sorry to disappoint those who were hoping to hear something gritty and sick, but there's nothing pathological here.

Just like I know I wasn't pathological, I know or can extrapolate that many others in interracial relationships have motives that are just as pure as or purer even than some of those in same-race marriages.

Posted by Evia at 7/04/2006 10:05:00
COMMENTS:
TP said...

Not sure if I can write on here as I'm not married yet. But I have noticed that there is always a "supposed" reason that people of different colours get together.

That whole status thing made my boyfriend laugh, as when I met him, he was working in a supermarket, living with his parents, had low self-confidence and no social circle to speak of. You find, as Halima says in her book, that people find it more comforting (even if offended) if there is some negative or calculated reason why the other race was chosen than the truth that you just found yourselves attracted to each other.

To an extent, I admit that I did initially go for a white guy because of my black ex-boyfriend, although I did get on well with him. I remember when he cheated on me. One of his excuses was, "It runs in my family," which was true to some extent as there were a lot of absent fathers and infidelities among the men of his family even though he was fairly middle-class. I did not feel it was a valid excuse but it did get me thinking.

Men of various colours have unstable childhoods and have experienced infidelity between parents and absent fathers. Although there is a higher rate of this in working class black communities in the UK, not to mention the black media at the moment and their portrayal of black men in relationships. I find and my friends have found that when asked, quite a few younger black men don't want to get married at all because, "*I haven't grown up with it and I haven't seen it around me.*" Then there are the ones that say they do want to settle down and be faithful but can't bring it into reality.

Maybe it's discrimination but I decided I was going to go for a white guy or a black guy with a bit more of a stable head on him and a learned respect for women. I knew I didn't want to go out with the same type I had before but I don't hate those men and I don't have a "preference" for white men as some people think.

All that said, you have to actually like someone and get along with him or her to have a real relationship.

Wed Jul 05, 10:51:00 AM EDT

Evia said...

Hi TP. It doesn't matter whether you're married to discuss this. Just feel free to say whatever. I'm just talking about interracial relationships from the standpoint of a married woman because I'm married. Some experiences may be different, depending on whether you're married or just dating. I don't know, but probably not by much.

So many people just don't seem to be able to wrap their brain around the notion that we were biologically females and males *before* we were ever politically defined as "black" and "white." Therefore, being of different genders, some of us of different skin shades and backgrounds or cultures are attracted to each other. Males and females are *wired* to be attracted to each other. Social conventions or social "*inventions,*" I should say, are not going to keep males and females apart. This is just not that complicated.

Wed Jul 05, 11:40:00 PM EDT

Free said...

I'm over here just rolling, Sis. I've heard people use all those negative notions you mentioned when talking about interracial relationships. (I am "auntie" to bi-racial children, so I've probably heard the same mess you have.)

Maybe when you get sick of waiting for people to get a clue & realize you married for love, you can just mess with their heads and agree with them: "Yeah, girl, I just didn't want babies with no nappy hair!" (While they're standing there with their mouth hanging open, you can leave. LOL).

Tell you what: I ain't hating on you for your love. I'm jealous as hell, but I ain't hating! Peace

Thu Jul 06, 03:07:00 AM EDT

Halima said...

Hello, it's Halima again. I'm totally behind your idea of communicating through a book, magazine etc. etc. It's not easy but it is needed because the voice of 'reason' and objectivity needs to penetrate and become a perceptible one. Right now, we have avoidance, dishonesty, denial, and the unreasonable and unrealistic voices dominating the debate, which lead many black women against their own interests!

I remember coming across a book while I was preparing to write mine, which started quoting the disheartening statistics of how many black men were unavailable for black women. I remember thinking, ok this black woman (the author) is going to now (logically) suggest black women try looking wider, but oh no, she went right back to advocating that black women 'compete' for the small pool of black men, and went on to set out 'rules' on how one could get the 'edge'.

I mean how dishonest and un-sisterly can one get!

I concluded then that some black women must surely have a very low opinion of us black women and see themselves as subordinate in the scheme of things, to be so 'uncharitable' towards us in this way.

Yes, you will sometimes find that the people you most want to help, i.e. black women, are the ones who will 'reject' you in the most disheartening way, but you keep plodding on and you will find allies in the most unusual places e.g. genuine black brothers, who are not interested in 'getting the better' of their sisters' 'blindness around relationships. http://www.dateawhiteguybook.com/

Thu Jul 06, 07:02:00 AM EDT
Evia said...

Free, you're just crazy! LOL! I might just do what you suggest and leave some mouths hanging open one of these days.

One day, my husband and I were walking down the street in Baltimore holding hands (since he loves holding my hand when we're walking anywhere) and as we approached a group of homeless black men, they got real quiet. As we passed, one of them started yelling over and over. "She jus witcha for yo money! She jus want yo money!"

My husband and I had talked about how we should respond to possible hecklers and such early on in our relationship and we had decided not to get stressed by other peoples' hang-ups about us, so we ignored this character and just kept on strolling. BTW, this hardly ever happens—only maybe 3 situations that I could call "incidents" since we've been together.

In the beginning, we got the "stares" but not so much anymore. I've learned that not all the stares are negative. Some people have told me they actually admire us and wish they had the nerve to cross that racial "line." I think the stares have lessened to an extent because of the prevalence of the bm-ww variety of interracial relationships.

Anyway, the incident was hilarious, but it ticked me off too. It also tugged at my heart. This homeless guy was acting out his own anger at black women (for whatever reason) and was thus trying to make trouble for me by planting suspicion in my husband's mind to make him see me as a gold-digger. On the other hand, he was hating on my husband for being white and "rich," or so he thought, or 'de evil white man.' Unreal!!

Evia said...

Halima! You found my blog. Great!

I agree with all you say. Black women had better start talking out about this 'taboo' subject of being *un-partnered* and start looking at non-black men as simply *more* men to add to their dating and marriage pool because the silence is killing us in various ways. Just look at the horrific health statistics on African American women. I don't know how other black women, like those in the UK, fare, but every time I read another abysmal health report about black women here, I connect it to the wretched aloneness, unsupported, unprotected, under-appreciated, devalued, and unloved status I see etched on the faces of many bw here.

I mean, it's common sense that anyone who has a loving and supportive mate is just going to be less stressed, more satisfied, and therefore healthier in general. There is an almost direct connection between the state of one's mind and their body. This is why my blog is devoted to urging bw to find the most loving, lovable, suitable, and compatible mate of whatever skin shade just as most sensible women among other groups of women in the world do.

What my sisters need to realize is that a "good" man is just that, *a good man*. At the end of the day, a man's skin shade does not determine that he will love and be good to you or NOT.

By being what they consider *loyal* to the race or to African American (AA) men as they wait for their "Mr. Right" bm, many AA women are simply sacrificing themselves for very admirable and lofty reasons, but AA men, for the most part, are not *showing* bw anywhere near this level of loyalty or that they love and appreciate bw. Therefore, I'd like for AA women to know they have choices in men of all skin shades and cultural backgrounds, and they can still pursue virtually all of the same activities, and maybe even more varied ones, with a non-black man as their committed mate. I do this myself, and I see other bw in interracial relationships doing the same thing.

As I read somewhere recently, 'white men with black women don't tend to be KKK members.' LOL! That is so basic, but it escapes many people! Many of the white or other non-black men who commit to bw are also totally open to being involved in a positive way in the black community, so I can't imagine that many of them would even try to prevent their black wife or girlfriend from being involved in the black community, if that's what she wants to do. The main point I'm making is there is no reason why a black woman with a non-black man cannot live as usual—participate in the same activities, have the same friends, work to uplift her community, *if* she chooses, in any number of the same ways that she would if her man were black.

2

A Good Mate Can Be Any Skin Shade

July 5, 2006, 9:30 p.m.

I find it beyond interesting that some black men tend to think that the sole reason I married a white man was for *his money*. My husband is comfortable financially, but he's certainly not rich. Not all white people are rich, just like not all black people are poor. Duh! People sure do live and breathe these stereotypes!

The thing is that many black men can't believe or don't want to believe that a white man can offer a black woman anything aside from money. That is just limited and wishful thinking. LOL! I also didn't marry my husband, Darren, because I couldn't get a black man. I simply met my husband first. I may have met a similar black man a day later, two weeks later, a year later, 3 years later, 8 years later or maybe 15 or 20 years later, or maybe in another life. At any rate, I wasn't about to wait. Has any reputable mathematician calculated how long a black woman should wait to meet a suitable black man while she allows favorable opportunities with other men to pass her by?

I've also heard some black women say that they can't have a white mate because he won't be able to relate to the ins and outs of the 'black experience,' which means racism, the way a black man can or will. Though this may be less likely, it is also somewhat stereotypical and wishful thinking because some black men either can't or don't want to relate to their black wife's situation if she's getting kicked in the butt by racism. The black husband of a good girlfriend of mine, for ex., wouldn't allow her to talk about the never-ending episodes of discrimination at her workplace. He would cut her short by saying something like, "Are you talking about that again?" or "Don't you ever get tired of talking about that?" That was so frustrating for her!

A few years back, I went through a bout of unfair racial treatment with a white supervisor at work. I talked with my husband about it throughout the whole stressful time I was going through it. Though he had never experienced *racially* unfair treatment, he has experienced unfair treatment. Therefore, he could and did empathize and support me emotionally and otherwise during this ordeal because he saw the situation as being a part of the legacy of the power differential between white males and others in the United States. The white male supervisor was simply taking advantage of the historic power embedded in the role of the white male. Therefore, my husband helped and supported me as I essentially reduced the power of the supervisor in this situation, and things turned out fine for me.

The bottom line is that a good husband is a loving mate, and he will somehow find a way to understand and support a woman he loves. It doesn't matter whether they share the same racial, cultural, or religious background.

Posted by Evia at 7/05/2006 09:52:00 PM

COMMENTS:
Free said...
You know what the deal is? You got a good man & your girlfriend got a dud. Both come in all races.

I dug your comment so much, I had to go and do another little post! I'll be over here catching your updates.

Keep doing your thing. Peace

Thu Jul 06, 03:01:00 AM EDT

Halima said...
Hello Evia, it's Halima here from the other side (ha-ha).

Just wanted to give you thumbs up for the blog. And you have made a particularly important point about the reasons black women dismiss other options. I commented about this also in my book.

There are a number of 'received wisdoms' we as black women have about interracial dating, and these can be very effective in getting us to dismiss other races of men, for two reasons: they somehow *sound logical* on the face of it, and in addition, it is impossible to test them out unless you are 'in' the relationship itself.

If a woman says to me, "I dated a white man and he couldn't understand me," I would respect that, because it is a real experience, but most of the women who come out with this reason number 1 for dismissing white men, haven't even shared their coffee break with one! So how can they be sure and emphatic this will be the deal, if they date white men. Truth is, they can't!

I must say that after 5 years of research for the book, I concluded that most black women in interracial relationships receive a 'satisfactory' level of support from their non-black spouses.

I am not saying these men know every 'in and out' as you so succinctly put it, but they are able to offer adequate comfort, support, a listening ear, encouragement, helpful ideas and a sounding board for their black partners. Indeed, what else would one be requiring?

I am a woman and I don't expect a man to know the ins and outs of my experiences as a woman, but I expect a 'satisfactory' level of support from any man I am involved with. He doesn't need to be a woman like me to be 'clued up'.

(http://dateawhiteguy.blogspot.com)

3

Don't Hate Me Because I Married a Good Man

July 8, 2006, 4:58 p.m.

I'm still trying to fully process a couple of disturbing, candid discussions I've had with girlfriends over the years when they've revealed to me some level of resentment regarding my *happily married with wonderful well-adjusted children* status. Just sharing here: I'm in my 2nd marriage now; my ex-husband (a black man) and I got divorced because he and I wanted to go in very different directions in our lives, but we are still good friends.

What really bothered me the most about the tirades of two of these women is that they've somehow *blamed* me for having found higher quality men to date and marry than they've been able to find. Was this my fault? They even bristled that my children are not among the negative statistics of black youths. Actually, these "friends" should be congratulating me and should feel very happy for me. (smh) Some people have labeled this phenomenon among blacks the 'crabs in the barrel' syndrome, or in general, I guess this falls under the heading of 'misery wants company' among human beings, overall.

Honestly, I did have some odd guilt feelings because it was almost like they felt I had unfairly gotten *privileges* that they had been denied: the *formula* for finding and selecting better quality men and raising more successful children. There was bitterness in their tone that I was somehow not sharing the formula with them.

Well here goes, folks: Part 1 of my *formula* is that I always use my head much more than my heart when making major decisions and that leads right into Part 2, which is that I never limited myself to AA men or black men.

Anyway, I actually did wonder momentarily, after each tirade, whether I'd kept something not so obvious from them. Crazy, right? However, after those initial feelings of unease, I sloughed off any responsibility for their unhappiness. On this blog site, however, I will elaborate on my *formula* for finding two quality, loving, lovable, suitable, and compatible men who wanted to commit to me.

I decided to avoid the façade of friendships with women such as these in the future because I don't know where to go with this type of relationship. I don't want them peeking into my life and getting angry at me when they compare themselves to me. Until they can raise their consciousness and grow in this department, I'm just not seeing how there can be any expansion in their lives or in their relationship with me.

I'm sad that they can't find a good man. If they'd been able to do so, maybe they and I would still have the type of friendship where our families could get together and do things like go on vacations together and grow old together as couples who've been friends for many years sometimes do. As things stand, these single women sometimes feel even more alone when they're with me and my husband. They're attractive, nice, and accomplished women. Many men would ordinarily be interested in them, but that's just not the case for many black women in the U.S. these days. This is, in part, because many black women consciously and subconsciously shun many non-AA men, especially if they're not black. In other words, many black women limit themselves to African American men or black men only. I have never done that.

I sometimes now don't even want other black women I meet to know that I'm happily married. I'm definitely slow to reveal this to any new black female acquaintance unless she tells me first that she has a quality man in her life. Recently, I met an AA woman at a fabric store and we started chatting about our love of fabric and fibers. When she suggested that we get together sometimes and work on craft projects, I stalled and changed the subject. It was only after she revealed that she was happy with the man in her life that I invited her over.

It seems that a "good" man has become such a scarce commodity for some women (not just black women). I realize that many women of all groups are finding it a challenge to find that type of man, but for some AA women, it's especially tough.

For the purpose of this topic, I define a good man as a man who is potentially ready, willing, and able (emotionally, financially, and spiritually) to commit to a long-term relationship and all that it involves—with a woman, either now or in the not-too-distant future. Some black women have developed severe hunger pangs for a *good* man, which causes them, like my friends, to *"hate on"* other black women who have one. I even recently read an article in a major magazine about this "black man scarcity" on college campuses these days and the toll it takes on young black college women personally and on their relationships with each other.

I guess this all means that it's fine to tell women that we don't need a man to be content because we don't, but neither were most of us meant to be alone.

Posted by Evia at 7/08/2006 05:23:00 PM

COMMENTS:
Chr said...

Evia, as a BF in an interracial marriage to a WM, I can totally relate to your blog. It seems that we have a lot in common. My story is interesting because both of my brothers are also in interracial marriages. It wasn't planned but just worked out that way. Needless to say, we have some interesting family gatherings. Looks like a UN meeting!

Sat Jul 08, 09:18:00 PM EDT

Evia said . . .

Girl, I know you can relate! The thing is that so many people think that it's about the "white," but I just wanted a man I could trust, love, one who would love me and bring enough to my table and treat me like I am special. Simple, huh? This stuff has become like rocket science to some men, based on what I hear from some sistas.

As soon as an AA woman mentions that she wants a man to bring "enough" to the table, a lot of AAs think she's talking about money. Not the case with me although a man's got to bring enough money to the table, because no one can live off air, but money is not the king to me.

My husband makes me feel special in lots of small ways. He tries hard to satisfy particular wants and needs of mine, and does special things like thinking of all kinds of ways to surprise me and endear himself to me. It always amazes me how he "listens" to me when I think out loud sometimes about things I want to do, places I want to go, or things I want done and the next thing I know, he's already made preparations to go to that place or do the thing I mentioned. This makes me feel appreciated and important in his life.

He also believes in equality in a relationship and doesn't care about traditional roles. Whatever I can do better, I do; whatever he can do better, he does. For ex. he's a fantastic cook! I'm not. We share the cooking ordinarily, either preparing meals together or taking turns on separate days, but whenever we have company, he mostly does the cooking. He doesn't care what people think about that traditional role "switch" because his masculinity is never in doubt by him or by me. He's a man who "thinks" for himself; one who is rarely swayed in his opinions or behavior by what other people think. I love that about him. I'm the same way.

Anyway, he's a great guy, but my first husband (a black man) was also a great guy. There are some really fantastic men out there—just not enough, and far too many African American women restrict themselves.

Chr said...

Anyway, he's a great guy, but my first husband (a black man) was also a great guy. There are some really fantastic men out there—just not enough.

> Are you sure we aren't related? My former husband, a black man (one of my very good friends to this day) is a great guy and a wonderful dad to my daughter, but he wasn't a good fit for me.

My husband treats me like a queen and knows how to make a woman feel cherished and appreciated. He is not perfect but I know he loves me and my daughter who affectionately calls him "Steppie".

My husband and I could have been the couple in the movie: "Something New." I am the uptight professional and he is the down-to-earth blue-collar guy. I could go on but I will take this to my own blog, which I will be starting soon!

Sat Jul 08, 10:38:00 PM EDT

Srejax said...

Evia, thanks for posting on an interesting topic. My boyfriend is white. He's the first non-black guy I've dated; I'm the first non-white girl he has dated. Our communication is great (usually), and we have the 'good, the bad, and the ugly' conversations about race. One of our more interesting conversations (and one that is ongoing) is his feeling that black women date white men because there aren't enough "good, black men." Clearly, that's not a great feeling for him—thinking that I'm "settling."

It's an interesting thought and conversation. I told him I could find lots of good, black men...just not ones who were good for me...or not as good for me as he is. Unfortunately, we as black women do tend to position our argument that way—that we only date white men because there aren't enough good black men. I guess that's how we justify it, which is probably interesting in that we feel a need to justify it...when very few other folks who date interracially feel a need to justify their decision.

I appreciate Halima's arguments on her website that black women need to really consider what is best for us individually. And my man—white and all-American as he may be—is best for me.

Anyway, keep posting!

Tue Jul 11, 10:13:00 PM EDT

4

The Mating War

July 6, 2006, 11:30 a.m.

On July 4th, we went to Philly for the parade and fireworks and to watch the performance of Lionel Richie and Fantasia on the Parkway there. Fabulous, hi-energy performance by Fantasia! OMG!

Anyway, I counted the number of IR couples as I sometimes do at gatherings. I counted 14 couples. Eleven were black men with white or white-skinned females and three were black women with white or non-black men. As usual, I also noted the number of women of all races and ethnicities who were unaccompanied by men, and black women easily won that distinction, as usual. Many black women were with other black women—whether girlfriends, same-sex s-o (significant others), or family members, I don't know. There were hordes of curvy, very attractive black women there—overwhelmingly not with men.

As it got later in the evening, those women who were with their husbands or boyfriends began to cozy up with each other. As a woman, I can just imagine how some of those unattached sistas felt.

Girlfriends are fun to hoot and holler with, but are absolutely worth zilch for cozying up.

I notice this a lot, no matter what social outing—lots of black women with each other—or by themselves. With such a large number of white and other non-black men in the U.S. who are single and potentially interested in bw, I know that some of those men would flock to bw—if they *believed* that bw were as receptive to them as Asian women are, for ex. It's very definitely the black community's condemnation of bw in IR's that's the main culprit keeping many of those women from giving white-skinned men the "green light."

Yes, I realize that some bw and wm are not attracted to each other for a variety of reasons, and yes, I know that *some* wm are not interested in a loving, respectable relationship with a bw, however many are or would be if they knew that bw were willing to explore the possibility. However, it's a fact that many of those black women who are interested in wm are afraid to give wm the green light because they feel they'll be accused by other black people of 'sleeping with the enemy' and/or of being disloyal to bm or labeled a "sellout."

The *disloyalty* factor is a biggie with African American women, or that "D" word. I experienced this 'enemy' accusation myself a few years ago when my husband and I were walking down the street, holding hands in a large urban area. A black man passing by looked me in the eyes and said, "Well, the Bible did say you're supposed to love your *enemy*." LOL!

I wonder if he says that to bm with non-black women. Nope. More than likely, he high-fives them or wants to congratulate them in some other way. Therefore, I know that some blacks consider me a "sellout" and a "traitor." These terms and accusations or similar ones are commonly pinned on AA women who date or marry interracially, but not on AA men. That's pure sexism.

It's obvious to me that many in the "black community" are very confused about a lot of things and are stagnated. Stagnated or lack of action often comes from stagnant/confused thinking. However, in any population of people who view themselves as being under siege (as some AAs do), there will be those who will think differently, break loose, and blaze a trail.

These people are usually more courageous (will act, despite fear), more adventurous, risk-takers. In nature, when certain environmental conditions are harmful or non-sustaining to any group of animals or plants, some of them will survive, but many will not. In order to survive, those survivor animals or plants have to go against the grain, either deliberately or accidentally.

In the realm of evolutionary science, this is *natural selection* in operation, or nature at work. In other words, nature will reward those animals or plants that are equipped (by whatever means) to survive a hostile or under-nourishing environment. Out of all the billions of plants, animals, and organisms that have existed since the beginning of time, the ones we see today are the offspring of the survivors. They're here because either an ancestor or they, themselves, most likely went against the grain at some point—either knowingly or not, and adapted to new environmental conditions. These survivors lived to reproduce progeny.

In the current 'mating war'—yes, it amounts to a war of competition—that African American women find themselves in, where we are competing for compatible, quality men with all the other women in the global village. Those black women, in particular, who go against the current hostile or under-nourishing grain, that makes up the lives of many AA women, are the ones who are most likely to successfully mate with males who will help them to produce the strongest and best equipped offspring for the future. It is the imperative of all living things to reproduce to avoid extinction, and as black women living in a hostile world, we should choose the best available male candidate (regardless of skin shade, race, culture, religion, etc.) to reproduce with—a male who will help us to protect and raise strong, well-equipped babies for the future. We cannot live in the past.

We live in the present and project ourselves into the future through our children. It didn't matter what complexion my babies were, or future progeny are, because I know I will be in their DNA— even if they don't have my skin shade. My complexion does not define me; it's just one tiny aspect of me.

COMMENTS:
Ruminations of a Racial Realist said...

Hey Evia, thanks for your comments on my blog. This is a great post. I must confess I am really confused about this topic at the moment. I need to do more reading and have more discussions about it. I've just discussed this issue by email with the author of a book on black women and relationships. She feels that it's ok for black women to date outside the race, but she's strongly against black men dating outside the race. I suspect that this is the conclusion I am going to come to as well.

I think the black woman-white man situation is totally different from the black man-white woman situation for all kinds of reasons. That said, I am a strong advocate of black-on-black love and I know that I personally would be best suited to a black man.

Thu Jul 06, 11:44:00 PM EDT

Evia said...

Ruminations, thanks for reading and commenting on my blog.

Yes, life used to be so much simpler. We tended to mate with the boy next door, so to speak. Today, things are lots more complex because the world has rapidly gone global and will never return to being a 'small-town' again.

I don't think most blacks I talk with (and others of all groups) understand all of the ways that we will have to change our thinking in order to survive and thrive in this new world. While we are still here discussing whether we should do this or that, the world is already moving on to the next level because change is a constant whether we can handle it successfully or not.

So many people are absolutely and stupidly focused on complexion and hair texture! I've always read a lot of evolutionary science material and these characteristics have virtually no intrinsic survival value for human beings in the 21st century. Isn't it totally amazing that even the best and brightest human beings—even some with so-called genius IQs—are fixated on these two characteristics? LOL!! This has happened solely because a few hundred years ago, greedy white slavers came up with an evil idea to invent "racial" categories. I'm sure that the individuals who spawned this idea never realized how that one idea would take the world by an evil storm. Wow! Just suppose you and I could come up with an idea that would have that impact on the world. Someone once said and I paraphrase, that 'nothing is more powerful than an idea—neither guns nor money.'

Anyway, IMO, black women are among the world's most desirable females and more and more men of all races and cultures are singing our praises. If we could only deal successfully with the self-esteem issues that plague some black women, I'm convinced that we would be on par to compete with all other women in the world for quality, compatible men. African American women lack self-esteem, by and large, because numerous AA men (with a lot of help from black women) don't place their stamp of approval on black female beauty and desirability the way that white and other men put it on their women's beauty and desirability. Anyway, I'll be talking more about this in my blog.

Fri Jul 07, 09:14:00 AM EDT

Meli said...

Hi, everyone, I am new to this blog site. Bravo site, Evia! This may be a bit off topic, but I really feel that black women should stop "playing" ourselves in relationships, which are going nowhere. Other ways that we decrease our desirability quotient is by having kids as teens and not taking advantage of higher education. Your tastes, experiences, education naturally place you into different social circles. Black men have been taking advantage of this for years. I don't understand how any BW these days can "fix her mouth" to say that she is only waiting on a 'brotha'. What?? Don't clamor and be desperate for any man!

Also, know that we are not the only women having to kiss some frogs before we meet the prince. Just watch the show "Cheaters" and many other media describing how immature men are doing women of all races wrong. Well, the women are behaving badly too and allowing poor treatment. As BW, let's focus first on our health! Heart disease is knocking us out left and right, diabetes too. Some of our habits are really hurting us.

I want to meet a man with my values and ideals and I feel that I will someday. I just don't put myself out there like I used to. Be careful whom you have kids with! I mean that no matter which race of man you choose. Make sure he is stable. Don't pay a man's bills! I work with a woman who brags daily that she is married to a 'brotha' and she bought him a cell phone and also pays his child support so that he won't go to jail. She does all of this on a Teacher's Aide salary of $17,000. But she brags that she is married! Any of us could be married tomorrow if we did not want to cultivate something worthwhile with a guy on the same page as us. Don't chase a man. We are not desperate!

I cannot be angry at BM anymore for their marriage choices when they continue to see images of WW and other women as more feminine, positive, etc. (the other list of stereo-types). I also don't like to read a great deal of literature on any form of the BWs woes and how no one wants us...Please! We must have better PR in the form of how we present ourselves.

A whole lot of us are still shy about being with a man of a different skin color, period.

Wed Sep 27, 08:10:00 PM EDT
Anonymous said...

I recently saw an episode of "Black Man Revealed" on TV One. One of the guests who was black stated that he hates to see a black women with a white man because he has images of them having sex and he also said that he felt that once a black woman starts dating a white man, he feels she will no longer date black men. He also said he dates white women but does not like black women to do the same. The other thing he said which was very interesting is he did not like the way black women act when with white men. He said they hold on to the white man. To me, he just described someone who was enjoying herself.

Sun Feb 25, 04:40:00 PM EST
Purple said...

I'm a white man, college educated, published author, working on a second degree, and still being rejected by most of the beautiful black women in my community. Black women are more beautiful, *yes* more desirable, and honestly, seem to be more up front about who they are and what they want when you speak to them. Unfortunately, most of them reject me because of my skin color. I usually ask a BW why—when she says no to a date, or when she can't ever make that second date, and they are usually honest about it.

Black women are truly beautiful, smart, strong willed and strong minded, and I grew up in a community that opposed interracial relationships. That does not stop me from my desires to be happy with good women. Who cares about the color!

Another point I realized was the attitude difference the black ladies would have when we got in the company of other black women and men. They were usually uncomfortable, did as little as possible to avoid being noticed, and usually came up with a reason for us to leave early. I felt dating outside their race brought them negative peer pressure from the men and the women of their own race.

Evia said:

> *I'm a white man, college educated, published author, working on a second degree, and still being rejected by most of the beautiful black women in my community. Black women are more beautiful, yes more desirable, and honestly, seem to be more up front about who they are and what they want when you speak to them. Unfortunately, most of them reject me because of my skin color.*

Welcome, and thanks for your comments, Purple. I know this happens, but many black women are "growing" rapidly in their consciousness in this area. In general, many blacks *and* whites have a lot of growing to do regarding this issue of *skin shade.*

5

Why Do People Ask Us How We Met?

July 24, 2006, 1:55 p.m.

People often ask my husband and me how we met. I don't know whether this is a common occurrence or as common for all IR couples, but it sometimes happens to us in the most surprising of places, like yesterday at a funeral for one of my husband's distant cousins. I was startled, to say the least, that anyone would be thinking about our racial differences at such a sad event, but the question popped out of the mouth of one of the bereaved as we conveyed our sympathies.

So, we stood there explaining how we met as others waited behind us on a long line to express their condolences. It was obvious why we were asked this question, but I thought it was very interesting how that could have even mattered to anyone at a time like that.

Another aspect of asking us 'how we met' is I've noticed that people tend to listen carefully to the answer. If we want to get total silence in a room, all we'd have to do is say, "Be quiet everybody because we want to tell you how we met." There are only a few things, that can get silence in a room as quickly as that, and I can't think of any of them now. LOL! We've even had people ask us the question twice, if we tried to ignore them the first time.

I've never cared that much how anyone met, and I've often wondered why exactly these people are interested in the details, of how we met. I definitely have my ideas about why they want to know, but when I've asked them, they usually grin and say, "Just wondering, that's all. " I'll bet volumes could be written on this.

Anyway, that's another thing—the grinning. People, especially white people over 40 or so, tend to grin at my husband and me a lot when we're out walking, dining, or even at a craft show. LOL! I'm not sure why. Verrry interesting. Anyway, one thing I can always say about my life as an interracially married black woman is that life is always way beyond interesting, to say the least.

Posted by Evia at 7/24/2006 02:17:00 PM

COMMENTS:
Angie said...

Hi Evia, as someone who is very curious about IRs (interracial relationships), I think I may be able to answer some of your questions. I think people may ask where you met because they want to know: *Where do you go to meet white men that want to date black women?* I know that sounds silly, but in this day and age where everyone says IR dating is okay, not everyone feels free to do it. Where is the place that made you both feel free to do the thing that many of the "askers" would like to have done.

I live in Columbus, Ohio, but I'm originally from New Orleans, Louisiana. You can't get any deeper south than New Orleans. I think my interest in IR couples began when I was young because of the Creoles and *passe blanc* people I knew growing up. At the root of their family history, there were IR pairings and they were not all forced through slavery. That peaked my interest, and I've been intrigued ever since.

By the way, how did you and your husband meet? LOL
Mon Jul 24, 04:44:00 PM EDT

Evia said...

LOL. I refuse to answer that question on the grounds that . . . Okay, here's the short version. We met at a crowded museum and he wanted to see me again. He e-mailed me, we communicated, and the rest is history.

Men are men and white men are no different. I've gone out with different races and ethnic groups of men since the time I began dating in my upper teens, and men are basically the same, except that in my experience, some men try harder to win a woman over. In my experience, African men and other men do this, too, except for when black women act desperate. I think AA women and other women here have *spoiled* many African American men, and that's why some of them act like they think they're the 'prize in the box.'

White men, I've noticed, don't tend to openly eyeball women and make moves on women the way a lot of black men in large urban areas do, and many white men are definitely hesitant about approaching a black woman because of cultural differences and the ongoing undercurrent of racial tension. Likewise, many bw don't give white men the green light, usually for the same or related reasons.

You might try the online route. Some white guys are definitely trying to meet bw that way and it would probably be a better way to ease into an IR relationship because you can screen him a lot better. I can't recommend any site, but there are a bunch of them on the internet. Just be careful about *any* in-person meeting with men who you meet online and follow *all* of the precautions. Women need to be careful about meeting men *anywhere*. Period.

Mon Jul 24, 08:17:00 PM EDT

Angie said...

Evia, your name is beautiful, btw.

I'm in a serious and loving relationship with a black man that I've known for quite a long time. So, I'm good. But I'm still intrigued by IRs. And I'm not sure why. As a junior in high school, I had a crush on a white guy. Well, we had a mutual crush. It didn't go much further because we were both afraid of what our families would think. (My mother did not approve, and I don't think his family would have either). As an adult, I've only been on one date with a white man, (living in Ohio). It did not go well, not because he was white, but because he was unsuitable for me.

So, after reading your posts and comments, I've begun to wonder why I am so curious about IR's. Is it because I grew up hearing that a white man could not really love a black woman in the same way a black man could? The 'romantic' in me has never wanted to believe that, so maybe I search for instances that disprove what I was taught. Or maybe I'm facing some of my own prejudices, because I'm not sure

I could truly love a white man without having some hang-ups about racial stuff. Hmmm, this is something to think about.

Hence the question, "Where did you two meet?" It's like asking, Where is that magical place that none of the s%#t that we have lived with for so long exists, and I can feel free to love a man, and not see his skin shade as a reminder of emotions and actions that are opposite of love. Feel me?

Tue Jul 25, 10:12:00 AM EDT

Anonymous said...

Very best site. Keep working. Will return in the near future.

Sat Aug 12, 03:56:00 PM EDT

Anonymous said...

This site is one of the best I have ever seen. Wish I had one like this.

Thu Aug 17, 07:44:00 PM EDT

6

Black Women—NEVER Accept Scraps!

February 19, 2007, 5:00 p.m.

    Here are a couple of pictures of Peter Norton (founder of *Norton Utilities*, now *Symantec*) with his wife, Gwen Adams. [See pictures at www.blackfemaleinterracialmarriage.com.] Gwen is another black woman who made a decision *not* to accept scraps.

    It all starts with making a decision. Gwen is a typical looking AA woman and so was Peter Norton's first wife, who was also an AA woman. We see black women who look like Gwen Adams every day. Yes, she's beautiful, but she looks very similar to many of the rest of us. Yes, she's intelligent. I'm sure that many of you are just as intelligent as Gwen. She's anatomically female. I *know* that all of the females reading this are made the same as Gwen, anatomically speaking.

    So, I want y'all to give some thought to some of the thinking and behavioral choices Gwen Adams probably had to make in her life prior to meeting Peter in order to meet him and be the woman in his life.

    I read that Peter Norton told *New Yorker Magazine* that he prefers black women. In other words, there is something that he finds in black women that he's not able to find in other women. Naturally, some people tried to say he has a *fetish* for black women—the usual stereotypical spin. Luckily, for him, since he's a mega millionaire, he is positioned so that he doesn't have to care whether people think he has a fetish or not. He and his first wife started a philanthropic foundation called the "Peter Norton Family Foundation" that has helped thousands of people over the years and naturally, his former wife, though divorced from him, is a very wealthy woman.

Don't sit around waiting on a relationship 'to happen' to you. Find out how you may need to change your thinking—the new thoughts you need to replace your current thinking with—and begin to think that way. After all, you *can* choose your thoughts and attitude in any given set of circumstances. If you continue to practice a new attitude, it will become a habit of mind.

Then *do* what you need to do to be in the orbit of your loveable and loving potential man, irrespective of his race, so that you two can find each other. Your man may not be a black man or a white man; he may be an Eskimo man, but in order to meet him, you're probably going to have to be in the vicinity of Eskimos—*if* no Eskimos are around you. So if you're not satisfied with the current crop of men around you, the question is what new decisions, choices, and actions are you going to have to make in order to change your circumstances?

Posted by Evia at 2/19/2007 05:35:00 PM

COMMENTS:
Keya said...
Amen. That is a beautiful couple, and the woman does look like the "average" black woman. She is not glammed up to Hollywood standards. So there are men out there for all of us.

Tue Feb 20, 12:34:00 AM EST
Anonymous said...
Well, if he marries her, let's hope she doesn't have a pre-nup!!! LOL!

Tue Feb 20, 05:59:00 PM EST
Ann said...
He loves black women. Obviously a man of good taste, excellent quality in women, and capable of seeing the profound beauty that is unique among black women. Hey, we are what we are.

Black women, the 'Crown Jewels' among all women. And I am

not ashamed to say that.
Phoenix_Sun said...

Evia, you have research skills that make the librarian in me very proud! Who would have known the Norton man who I have seen so many times on the Norton Antivirus CD-ROM's was into the sistahs. White America (along with the 'keeping-it-real'-black community) must not be very happy about powerful white men seeing black women as their ideal mates. If he slept with black women on the down-low, nobody would have a problem with it because that is a comfortable stereotype, but the fact he admits publicly to loving black women, marries them, or has long-term relationships with them must make a lot of people raise an eyebrow.

Tue Feb 20, 10:32:00 PM EST

Evia said...

> Evia, you have research skills that make the librarian in me very proud! Who would have known the Norton man who I have seen so many times on the Norton Antivirus CD-ROM's was into the sistahs. White America (along with the 'keeping it real' black community) must not be very happy about powerful white men seeing black women as their ideal mates. If he slept with black women on the down low, nobody would have a problem with it because that is a comfortable stereotype, but the fact he admits publicly to loving black women, marries them, or has long-term relationships with them must make a lot of people raise an eyebrow.

Phoenix Sun, actually there are readers who read my blog who keep me supplied with the pictures, videos, and article links. *They* are the master diggers for this material!

What you're saying is *so* true! We certainly don't typically see BW-WM couples being featured on "Entertainment Tonight," and I really believe that some people would *prefer* that this information is kept on the down-low. For example, bm have known for hundreds of years that white men were sleeping with bw, but it seems that certain bm get *really* upset when we walk out in public with wm or when wm marry us. I've had a couple of "edgy" experiences with black men in public when they see me walking down the street with my husband holding my hand. My husband loves to hold my hand when we're out walking just about anywhere—even when no one is around, but I can tell that bm really don't like that when they see us. As they say, "If looks could kill . . . ."

Tue Feb 20, 10:51:00 PM EST
Anonymous said...

May I say thank you for this blog, I understand if you need a break, but reading this has helped me look at myself differently, more acceptingly and lovingly. I am a 50+ divorcee (after 30 years of marriage to 'Mr. Wrong') who is trying to overcome feelings of rejection and to get rid of the "coping skills" I needed to stay married to a fool.

Also, when signing up for online dating, I wasn't comfortable listing other ethnicities as options. Now I have the courage to consider them and look past my preconceived notions, fears and prejudices to the possibility of finding my 'Mr. Exactly Right' to be a white man. What will Momma say? Thanks and God bless you!

Wed Feb 21, 10:39:00 AM EST
Felicia said...

You are correct, Evia. Most people, and certainly, many—if not most black men—would rather keep this information (and visual representation) regarding these high profile white men-black women couples on the down-low. For some reason, it seems like every society has a need to have some so-called "less than"/looked down upon/despised group at the bottom. I'm not just talking about Western societies but cultures as a whole around the world. In India, it's the *Dalits*/"Untouchables." In Japan, it's the *Burakumin*. In Hitler's Germany, it was the Jews. In Somalia, it's the Bantus. The list goes on. Well, IMO, in the African-American community, some black folks try to downgrade *certain* females.

Yes, some may say we're talking about sexism here but I really believe there is a racial element to it as well because if you look at who's upheld as the "true beauties" in the community, it's usually those of us black woman with lighter complexions and visible non-black ancestry. Whether it be hair-texture, skin-tone, features, etc... And regardless whether White men originally set this Euro ideal into motion, today it's Black men who perpetuate it in the media and the community at large.

Now how does all of this relate to the issue of white men-black women couples? IMO, since white men are socially and internationally considered to be at the top of the totem pole (especially those who are professionals and/or are very financially well off), when we're seen in their presence openly in a respectful and loving manner as spouses and significant others, we're no longer viewed as pariah. Then, the focus is shifted to who is the next group at the bottom. That group would most likely be black men because they're already in a precarious and compromised position.

Black men know this, and that's why some are hell-bent on destroying the self-esteem of weak, easily influenced/controlled black women who let them. That's why some black men continue to tell black women that a white man could never love them, respect them, and marry them. They do this in order to control bw and their behavior, thus giving these bm the only power the vast majority of them will ever get to experience in this lifetime.

Nobody in their right mind wants to be considered "on the bottom"/inconsequential. And this is the feeling/emotion that some (not all, thank God, as some are truly secure) black men experience when they see couples like us. They get a feeling that they've lost the one and only power (the ability to control our feelings and behavior) they ever had and will ever have—their power to rule over black women.

White women also don't want to give up their place on the pedestal. This is also a natural reaction to a feeling of loss. If the tables were turned and we women of color had their life experience—and they, ours—we would be the ones fighting to stay on top of the hierarchy.

Nobody wants to lose a sense of power, whether real or imagined. Deserved or not. And that's what makes the white male-black female open, loving, and respectful (especially legally recognized i.e. marriage) pairing so controversial, and thus hidden from public view in the popular media.

And that's why some folks of all colors 'trip' when they actually encounter us. It's like seeing the Loch Ness Monster or something! LOL People are caught off guard and a little scared because they have been purposely kept in the dark about our existence by the powers-that-be.

We cause folks to question tenets & ideologies fed to them since birth.

Wed Feb 21, 11:30:00 AM EST
Ann said..

> Nobody wants to lose a sense of power, whether real or imagined. Deserved or not. And that's what makes the white male/black female open, loving, and respectful (especially legally recognized i.e. marriage) pairing so controversial and thus hidden from public view in the popular media.

Well said, Felicia. Many people, and not just black men, want to keep black women's minds poisoned and polluted with the fear that white men only want us for sex. An intelligent and self-actualized, aware black woman can tell the difference between a fake man (of any race) and a real man (of any race).

And you are right about societies the world over needing someone to look down on. And some black men in America are no exception to this rule. They have known for so long that we black women would not run off into the arms of non-black men.

They have known that we black women are known for our legendary loyalty.

Misplaced loyalty.

Blind, stupid loyalty.

But, thank God, many black women are waking up, not to castigating black men whom they love and marry, but, black women are waking up to grabbing the gusto and giving themselves happiness in their lives.

No one else will do it for us, if we do not do it for each other.

On another note, I am kicking some butt in defense of black women on another blog.

And you guessed it. Yep, he's a black man. Sigh.

The defense and uplifting of black women never ends.

But, hey, I love a good challenge.

Especially when it is the honor, integrity and happiness of black women that is at stake.

Wed Feb 21, 02:33:00 PM EST

Zabeth said...

> That's why some black men tell black women that a white man could never love them, respect them, and marry them. They do this in order to control bw and their behavior, thus giving these bm the only power the vast majority of them will ever get to experience in this lifetime . . . . Nobody in their right mind wants to be considered "on the bottom" or inconsequential. And this is the feeling/emotion that some (not all thank God, as some are truly secure) black men experience when they see couples like us. They get a feeling that they've lost the one and only power (the ability to control our feelings and behavior) they ever had and will ever have—their power to rule over black women.

I once heard a BM say, about BW in interracial relationships, that he disliked seeing sisters with WM because WM have so much power: "They (WM) have all the jobs, all the money, all the power and it's like they're taking something else from me."

Not his exact quote. Nonetheless this really stood out in my mind. I still think about it to this day.

http://zabethblog.blogspot.com/

Evia said...

> On another note, I am kicking some butt in defense of black women on another blog.

LOL. I'm sure you would make a sista proud, wherever it is you're standing up for us, Ann!

But Ann, I hope you're also pointing those damaged black men over here to my blog. My site will shut them up like nothing else will because they will see here a sign of things to come. They will see that AA women can find men in the global village who do appreciate us to the max, if/when we decide to broaden our options—whether it's interracially or interculturally.

I do go to those sites sometimes—only to point the men and women over here. I would like for other black woman to do the same. This is very effective and empowering *Public Relations* that we're doing here for black women, y'all! Mail coming into my private mailbox and comments prove to me that this is working!

Also, we've got to be bold enough at every opportunity to stand up for young black girls and start molding them to broaden their options while they're still young—*before* they get filled with too many lies and get too scared and start feeling ugly, and unworthy. Other than that, many of them will become "practice" material for some of those sadistic black men.

Wed Feb 21, 03:38:00 PM EST

Evia said..

> *I once heard a BM say, in regard to BW in interracial relationships, that he disliked seeing sisters with WM because WM have so much power: 'They (WM) have all the jobs, all the money, all the power and it's like they're taking something else . . . .*

Well, wouldn't that make you think that more bm would treat black woman right, if they truly feel that way?

This is why a man has to *show* me that he's there for me. I don't want to hear sad sob stories because that's just all hot air! People are judged by what they *do*—not by how they *feel*.

What that guy said sounds to me like pure manipulation and an attempt to reinforce the loyalty chokehold bm already have on so many bw.

BW had better learn this lesson this time because if we don't, our girls will keep repeating it for generations to come.

Wed Feb 21, 03:49:00 PM EST

Anonymous said...

> *Well, if he marries her, let's hope she doesn't have a pre-nup!!! LOL!*

Are you saying we are gold-diggers? Don't worry. He will make sure she gets nothing; white men are sure to do that. As for black men, they usually let the white women get over on them—like NFL Strahan and the other guy. $15 million comes to mind. A black woman would never get that kind of a chance.

Wed Feb 21, 04:06:00 PM EST

Felicia said...

> But Ann, I hope you're also pointing the attention of those damaged black men over here to my blog—because this site will shut them up like nothing else will because they will see here a sign of things to come.

True that! LOL

I also strongly suggest that black woman strong enough to stomach some of the bull crap that is spouted on many of these black oriented message boards (I very rarely visit them because the atmosphere is often too insane) should *be sure* to direct those dudes over here—so that they can get a good earful and eyeful. This is a *new* age with new attitudes. It's clear that certain folks need to be brought up to speed.

And ditto everything you said about this young crop of young black girls. It is *vital* that they're molded positively before their self-esteem is destroyed and they become statistics.

> They (WM) have all the jobs, all the money, all the power and it's like they're taking something else from me.

Manipulation pure and simple. Actions speak louder than words.
Wed Feb 21, 04:33:00 PM EST

Evia said...

I didn't address the pre-nup comment, but I guess I should.

I don't think a woman who marries a very wealthy man should ever sign a pre-nup unless she is directed to do so by a very good lawyer because men and women *still* don't have equal opportunities in life and are still viewed *very* differently worldwide. It is *still* very much a man's world. Let's be real about that. If a woman in such a position doesn't protect her interests, she can be easily treated like yesterday's garbage, if the man wants to replace her.

My husband has some assets, but if he'd asked me to sign a pre-nup, I wouldn't have married him because that to me indicates a lack of trust. If someone obviously doesn't trust me, I don't trust them either. That's just me. So I would have walked away from the relationship.

We know it takes money to live well. I do think a rich man's money is a factor when a woman of lesser means considers marrying him. But I think that people have a tendency to totally disregard what she contributes to his life because they can't *see* what she gives him because women tend to be devalued in all societies. People instead look at the big house and the luxury items and lifestyle that his money provides. They overlook what she's giving him. I mean, he must be getting something from her that's valuable to him because otherwise he wouldn't want to be with her. He's getting *intangible* things from her that are obviously important to him, and this is what the court looks at and has to put a value on when the relationship crashes.

So I think she should get a fair amount of his assets if they part company. She should not sign her rights away because she doesn't know what she'll have to give him in the process of the marriage. Also, she can't afford to overlook other opportunities that she passed up while she was with him.

In my first marriage, I lived a very comfortable life—sort of like in a gilded cage. I worked because I wanted to. My money was all mine. My African husband was a workaholic and was an excellent provider. He was rarely ever home, but he knew he could trust me and could rely on me totally to manage the household and our lifestyle. That gave him tremendous peace of mind, so he could devote all of his time to his work. His career went through the roof! I had friends who were jealous of me because they looked at what he was providing materially and didn't see what I gave him.

Yeah, I had material things, but take it from me: those things alone don't make you happy. To this day, he praises me because of what I gave him.

Now, of course, we weren't nearly on the level of these multimillionaires. Those women have to deal with a lot! It's easy to say the women don't deserve those hefty settlements when you look at it from the outside. Some of those men are not nearly as nice as my ex-husband was. Some of those men are real SOBs! Most of the time, I think those women—whether they're black, white, or whatever—have earned every cent they get from those guys. I mean, some of those men figure they've bought and paid for those women. So you can just imagine what happens behind closed doors when a man thinks he's bought and paid for you! Many times, those women are treated like decorative *objects*.

Anonymous said...

I agree with everything that has been stated here. I'm a black woman married to a black man and we have two daughters that we have raised to be open-minded in their dating preferences. I know that you're shocked that my black husband would go along with something like this but unlike most black men, he isn't walking around with blinders on.

We have always encouraged our daughters in everything—from their education to their morality, so why should this be any different? We have told them that they can be just about anything they want to be in life so why discourage them from seeking happiness with a non-AA male just to make the black community happy and them miserable? My husband is Jamaican and their way of thinking is way different from the black men in America. He has no sympathy for American black men, whatsoever.

Thu Feb 22, 01:16:00 AM EST

Zabeth said...

On the pre-nup issue, I personally wouldn't advise against it, as long as it's fair to you as well! Everyone's definition of fair is different. I wouldn't be opposed to signing one as long as I had a qualified lawyer review it and my interests were represented too. I don't think a pre-nup necessarily means that the two of you are apprehensive about the stability of your relationship. Things just happen in life.

They're so common nowadays that even the average Joe seems to want to have a pre-nup; some women even ask for them. Then again, I do live in Los Angeles (LOL!). There is always the post-nup too. Moreover, no agreement is ever iron clad. Just ask Ivanna Trump, K-Fed, and Jessica Simpson.

Thu Feb 22, 03:23:00 PM EST

Anonymous said...

All I can say is thank God for women of all colors. Thanks for opening my eyes to this PR campaign. This explains all the *mean muggins* [frowns] and grunts I get from you BW in the streets. I guess the BM has one more thing to look over his shoulders for in America. I hope to God you *do not* have sons. Unfortunately, they will be BM too because of your God given dominant genes. What a waste.

Tue Feb 27, 09:25:00 PM EST

Anonymous said...

Maybe if BW did not have a fascination for thugs and criminals, we would not be in this situation today. You date them, have kids for them and finally want a "nice man" when you pass 30 or so. ummm...ok.

Tue Feb 27, 09:28:00 PM EST

Anonymous said...

Maybe if the black "men" who abandon their black children every damn day of the week actually stayed to help raise them they wouldn't turn out to be thugs and criminals to begin with.

And there are plenty of black women who wouldn't give a thug or a criminal the time of day. But I do agree that when you make your bed hard, you'd best be content to lie in it.

And thank GOD for real men of all colors. It's good that eyes are being opened to the growing number of black women expanding their choices in the dating and marriage department. The only BM who have to "look over their shoulders" these days are the ones who are up to no good to begin with.

This blog is not about *dissing* black males as a group. Instead, it's about pointing out negative behaviors and attitudes and teaching black women to love themselves and avoid this specific predator type of male. Whatever color/"race" he comes in.

And rest assured, there most certainly are contributors to this board who have sons. Many of our sons are being raised to be wonderful, strong, loving, and intelligent young men—not only by their mothers but also their fathers.

Our sons are being raised to be contributing members of society, free of the paranoia, worthlessness, and misogyny crippling some of the "brothas" out there.

Again, the only black men who could possibly be threatened by this wonderful and inspiring blog are those who are suffering from some of the very issues we discuss here frequently.

If the shoe fits, wear it. And if it doesn't, there's nothing to worry about.

Thu Mar 01, 03:50:00 PM EST

7

Anger is for Losers

January 10, 2007, 2:45 p.m.

I went to the bank this morning to discuss a special type of account that is connected with my home business, so I had to speak with a bank officer who turned out to be a white male, who was around my age.

We started talking—about the pros and cons of various types of business accounts and such—all quite formal and the usual stuff. He was reasonably attractive and very well- groomed, as you'd expect from a bank officer. Suddenly, I thought about some of the black women on my blog here who continue to say that white males don't show interest in black women and I decided to do an experiment.

I became chatty, friendly, threw in some wit, and smiled whenever it was appropriate. At a certain point—maybe 5 minutes into the discussion, I became aware that his manner had changed. He was now very talkative, warm, humorous, and began to dig for information for me on his computer. He went on and on explaining many features of various accounts and details to me, and suffice it to say that I knew he was going just a tad beyond the call of duty, so to speak. He was becoming more interested in me, as a person—not just a bank customer. He actually found a way for me to get me an account without paying fees. Yippee! Anyway, he then asked me my name.

I became a bit closemouthed at this point because my experiment was getting out of control. I wondered what my name had to do with anything, but I also realized that he was responding to my friendliness and men love friendly women. I told him my first name, stood up to leave, and thank him for the info. He asked whether I was local. I told him I was. He then wanted to know my last name and he wrote down my first and last name, saying he wanted to put some notes in my account. I gave it to him, but at this point, I knew I had to get out of there. He gave me his card and shook my hand. When I left the bank, I knew without any doubt that this guy was going to get into my account and get the whole scoop on me.

Now, I wasn't dressed up or anything—just had on jeans, a plaid shirt, windbreaker, and since it was windy here today, my hair was looking wild. I didn't have on makeup except for a little lipstick and the only thing that may have been a little unusual about me is that I was wearing some of my jazzy, long earrings that I made. As I drove off, I tried to see myself through his eyes. I guess I'm average, on the slimmer side, well-spoken, and I'd been very friendly.

I definitely knew that something about our interaction had perked his interest. I didn't have up any wall. I treated him exactly the way I'd treat any man who I felt comfortable with because I had felt very comfortable with him. After all, white men are just men like any other man. If they're uncomfortable around me; I'm uncomfortable. If they're relaxed, I'm relaxed. Not once did I think of him as 'de evil white man' because I don't think all white men are evil or responsible for white supremacist structures in our society or world. All white men benefit from the racist structures in place, but some of them wouldn't go over the edge if the structures disappeared. They were all born into these structures and they take the handouts they're given for granted, but they're not all equally invested in maintaining these unjust structures.

Let's be real: some black women harbor palpable anger towards *all* white men. I'm not saying it's not justified to be angry about racism, but it's not logical to be angry towards all white men. This doesn't help the situation at all. Actually, it's not only *not* beneficial; it's unhealthy and uses up a lot emotional energy. It would be different if the anger was being channeled to accomplish a positive goal, but

I don't see that happening in any angry black woman I know of or know.

On the social front, it turns many black women into shrewish 'Sapphires' and puts them at a major disadvantage when it comes to relating to men. While they're being angry at white men and sometimes black men, other races and ethnicities of women are being friendly towards all groups of men—giving these men the green light (as I did for a few minutes with the bank officer). Remember that men are not attracted to angry women—no matter how justifiable their anger may be. Likewise, I, for one, am not attracted to angry men and have always steered clear of them.

However, when these same angry black women see men with these other women, that makes them even angrier, and the cycle continues. In this way, the anger and 'closed' (thanks again to IR blogger, Halima, for that term) posture of many black women actually help other women to get quality black, white, and other men because so many black women take themselves out of the competition for these men. For ex. if many other black women had been receptive to Darren before he met me, it's possible he would have been with another black woman at the time we met because there are many black women in the environment where he works.

Black women need to realize that the world is not going to miss a step because they're angry. The world doesn't care. So at the end of the day, black women need to ask themselves: what good is my anger doing me and actually write out a list of the pros and cons if you need to see how illogical and what a waste it is. However, if you discover that your anger is an asset, that's the only time you should hold onto it. Otherwise, there are ways to get rid of it.

Also some of us need to brace ourselves for Valentine's Day and other 'special' occasion days for loving couples because those seem to be desolate days for many AA women who don't have a loving man. It's even hard for those of us who have loving men in our lives because we have to be careful to keep the details of what our men gave us for Valentine's Day, what we did for him, or where we went, etc. from black women who are alone. So, it's 'on' for that day because some black women *hate on* each other a lot—for being in a loving relationship with a good guy!

Anyway, in 2008, I think all black people should know black history from A to Z, if possible, and be extremely proud of our history, our contributions to this country and the world, our courage and our strides in this country, but we can't undo history. IMO, AA women, in particular, need to work hard to make whatever adjustments are necessary to get themselves into a position of comfort or at least a *more* comfortable position, so that they and their children are not in the negative statistics or suffering category to such a high degree.

There are various ways of doing this. Mating with or marriage to a better quality man is not the only way, but it is within reach of many more women than some of the other ways. As quiet as it's kept, some women in this country and throughout the world continue to see marriage as a way to elevate themselves. And having children outside of marriage is just a big-time no-no when you consider the heavy financial and emotional investment that's needed.

Posted by Evia at 1/10/2007 03:10:00 PM

COMMENTS:
Heavenly Zeta said...

I left anger alone a long time ago. It's really not good for your spirit. And you are right, Evia, when you say "The world doesn't care". That's what I tell my friends, my clients, all the time. And men literally *run* away from angry women. No matter why she might be angry, all he envisions is that anger being turned in his direction, and he will simply move on and find a woman who isn't. Some black men try to use that "Angry black Woman" stereotype to justify why they have opened up to women of other ethnicities. We'd do ourselves a world of good (and make folks wonder) if we (black women) would do a complete 180 in regards to our attitude...

Evia said...

> *And men literally run away from angry women. No matter why she might be angry, all he envisions is that anger being turned in his direction, and he will simply move on and find a woman who isn't. Some black men try to use that "Angry black Woman" stereotype to justify why they have opened up to women of other ethnicities. We'd do ourselves a world of good (and make folks wonder) if we (black women) would do a complete 180 in regards to our attitude...*

Well said, Heavenly Zeta. This is why I continue to say that we black women need to keep on our 'thinking caps' and adjust those caps from time to time because some of what we're doing now is just not logical and is creating the opposite of what many of those women want. Embracing *all* black men—some of whom are outright disdainful and predatory in their behavior towards us—is extremely foolish and not logical to me, and shunning a whole group of men—some of whom might be interested in loving us—is also counterproductive and ridiculous. So many missed opportunities!!

However, most of what AA women do is 'on point' and as a group, we get big kudos for this far and wide. It's just in the male-female relationship area that some of us are off base. Most of us grew up vaguely thinking that we would have a black mate because that's the way the racial situation is framed in this society, but since that may not be the case for many black women, they must adapt to 'different' conditions. That's another thing: Different seems to be often viewed as scary or negative, but different is not actually negative in most cases; it's simply different. LOL! I like 'different.' It doesn't scare me; it's just another slice of life.

Obviously some bw are not cut out for a 'different' relationship with a white man or even a black man from another country. Remember that some AAs discourage intercultural relationships too. I was criticized for marrying my first husband, a Nigerian. Black folks here would say stuff like, "Why isn't an AA man okay for you?" Lawdy!

It's just fine if an AA man is a black woman's preferred man, but she shouldn't allow him to lessen her life simply because he's from the same-race or culture—out of any 'loyalty to the bm' thing. That's the part that a lot of AA women never hear. They're often pressured to put up with poor treatment from an AA man, simply because he's black and from the same ethnic group. It's either that or she's supposed to have no man at all. AA girls and women are still being hit with these messages constantly; whereas 'loyalty' to AA women is not drilled into AA men by older AA men on anywhere near the same level. So the men come up with all kinds of silly excuses to abandon the women and children.

I find it interesting that many bm who do this know they're not respected by other men in the world for this abandoning behavior because a man who deliberately abandons his family, his children, is worthless in the eyes of most real men in the world. This is why *some* AA men have mounted a massive campaign to denigrate bw to make us seem like we're unappealing, impossible to live with, and have all kinds of major issues.

This just crushes a lot of AA women because the women don't see that this is mostly just a cover up for the inadequacies of these males. Also, a typical bw knows when the bm is making excuses, whereas a typical non-bw doesn't know it. This type of ignorance (not knowing, on the part of the non-black woman) is bliss for these men.

Let's face it—if men around the world abandoned their women and children simply because the women had "issues," or flaws, human beings would be extinct by now. Of course, I realize that some AA women have *issues,* and I've encouraged bw to work on the 'anger' issue and others, and be their best in every way. But come on! Raise your hand if you know that other groups of women also have some of the same *issues.* And why is it that a typical man from other groups can have a successful relationship with the same type of AA woman that a bm here would say is "too strong?"

See, it's just clear to me that black men here are just trying to cover up their inadequacies by blaming it all on the black woman by blowing every molehill or wart in an individual AA woman's personality into a mountain. It's just a cover.

As a black womanist, I will always encourage and support a black woman finding whatever works best for her.

Wed Jan 10, 08:14:00 PM EST

Chr said...

I remember when my husband and I first started dating and he said, and I quote. "You are the most atypical black woman I have ever met." I had to ask what he meant. Since he had not dealt with black women on a personal level, he had just seen them on TV—the loud Sapphire/*Boomquisha* types—angry at the world and not afraid to show it. All men want is a place where they can feel comfortable and accepted. A peaceful place. Take a note from Delilah. She had Samson so comfortable that he gave up the key to his strength.

Wed Jan 10, 08:55:00 PM EST

Ann said...

> *the loud Sapphire/Boomquisha types.*
> *'Boomquisha.'*

Ha! Ha! Funny. I agree. The anger only eats you up inside and hurts no one but you.

As I was growing up, my mother was my idol in how she interacted lovingly with my father. I always wanted to be like her in her showing of love, loyalty, and support towards my father while he was alive.

Any man who is married to a woman wants to come home to a life of peace and comfort after fighting all the hells of the outside world. And women want the same too.

While growing up, I read many works of fiction and none had the greatest effect on me as the story of Ulysses and Penelope. We all know of Ulysses who went off to fight in the Trojan War. For 20 long years he was gone, and Penelope, his queen/wife stayed steadfastly loyal to him until he returned. Twenty years. Okay, I have 10 years over her, but, the gist of what I am trying to say is that cultivating loyalty, good graces, and an inviting demeanor can and will attract a person to you. Yes, we women can all have bad days, and who doesn't? But, I find that what makes my day more pleasant is when I smile and say "Hello," to any man I pass while going about my day. And not just black men. All men.

Yes, some of them seemed shocked, and I guess the "Boomquisha" syndrome has something to do with that. But, I know it doesn't take much to smile; it uses less facial muscles than frowning, and it certainly keeps your blood pressure down and your spirits up.

My goal is to be a lot less reserved which to many people can come off as stuffy and uptight. But once many people have gotten to know me, they all exclaim, "Hey! You know, you're a real fun, nice person. I'm glad I got to know you better."

On another note. Went to the theater today with the intent to see "Dreamgirls". Paid for the ticket, movie was to start at 12:30PM. To while away the time, I went to go see "Children of Men." Stayed and watched that wonderful movie. I highly recommend all of you go see this movie. It has a message that needs to be realized, and it's also a great film starring one of my favorite actors, Clive Owen.

Movie ended and I saw the time of the next showing of "Dreamgirls," realized it would start too late for my tastes, went to go see "The Good Shepherd," starring another one of my favorite actors, Matt Damon. (Oh boy, he is a hunk, but then again he's from Texas like me, what can I say—Texas has the best looking people in all the

50 states at least in my humble opinion, but I digress.) This movie was also good.

Anyway, I did not get to see "Dreamgirls," but at least they got the proceeds from my ticket purchase. Hopefully tomorrow if all goes well, I will go back to see it. It is showing on two screens with at least 8 showing times between both screens.

Wed Jan 10, 09:22:00 PM EST

Meli said...

Boomquisha! LMAO! That is hilarious, Chr!

Good post Evia, I like this post about how anger does us no good at all. All too many times at work, I see BW (sad, but true) coming to work with nasty attitudes trying to intimidate everybody. It's quite unfair that some of us make outward expression of anger our mantra of sorts.

Some of us are even defined by anger. How many times have you heard others of us state that "so and so is just so mean and hateful" or "so and so won't take no s#@*!" It's stated in a way that actually praises this type of behavior. Truly successful people know how to control their anger, or they use bits of it to get ahead.

On a different note, I want to introduce another option/cyber venue in which to meet interested men. Craigslist, is like an online personals page. All of the major cities use it from everything to apartment hunting, jobs, to dating. It is Craigslist.com and I browse many ads in all the major cities to check out whose interested...kind of like a project. LOL!

Wed Jan 10, 09:57:00 PM EST

Zabeth said...

Hi Evia! Thank you sooooooooooo much for this post. It's definitely a wakeup call.

On an aside, I think some BW do use their anger as power; it becomes an asset. Speaking from experience, when I was younger (as in early 20s), I'd throw a "tantrum" to get my way and, it would work. I'd get my way because nobody wanted to deal with me. Also, I think it's much harder for BW to release some of that anger because their anger is constantly being reinforced.

Wed Jan 10, 09:59:00 PM EST

Evia said...

> *Some of us are even defined by anger. How many times have you heard others of us state that "so and so is just so mean and hateful" or "so and so won't take no s#@*!" It's stated in a way that actually praises this type of behavior. Truly successful people know how to control their anger or they use bits of it to get ahead.*

Meli, this is so true! Some black women play that shrewish 'Sapphire' role to the hilt and wear it like a badge of honor. They get all kinds of praise for "telling somebody off" or "going off on" somebody, and this is certainly one reason why they continue to do it. It's tragic how so many dysfunctional behaviors that black people display is considered "acting black" and "keepin' it real." LOL! This is why it's so important for people to know their history. Many black women have no idea they're still playing a role learned from their ancestors, that was imposed by that former slave system.

They think they *'don't take no s%$t'* when actually they've taken something that was derived from the slavery period and perfected it!! As I said in one of my blogs a couple of weeks ago, the 'Sapphire' (stereotyped as the loudmouth and tough-as-nails verbally-vicious black woman) was one of the 3 major roles historically assigned to black women and many bw embraced that role just like many bw embraced the *Mammy* role.

The Sapphire and the Mammy are deeply embedded in AA culture. And when some of us say that AA women have got to stop mammying and acting like Sapphires, many other black women and men go ballistic, sometimes because they really believe this is a part of our "authentic black" selves, when nothing could be further from the truth. I hear black folks many times say something like: "Leave that girl/woman alone. You're trying to make her act like a passive, timid white girl/woman." At the same time, isn't it interesting that many bm say now that the passive, more timid type of woman is the type they want? Boing!!! LOL!

Wed Jan 10, 10:23:00 PM EST

Evia said...

Yes, Zabeth, tantrums are attempts to grab power. Hope you' ve grown out of that behavior.

> On an aside, I think BW do use their anger as power- it becomes an asset. Speaking from experience, when I was younger (as in early 20s), I'd throw a "tantrum" to get my way and, it would work. I'd get my way because "nobody wanted to deal with me"
> Also, I think it's much harder for BW to release some of that anger because their anger is constantly being reinforced."

In such a place as this country, things are not often what they seem to be. If you mean that the anger is reinforced because so many anti-bw messages constantly make black women angry, then I agree. However, anger is a choice. Many black women have never learned to react in alternative ways or less destructive ways to the various anger triggers or learned to not allow certain situations to trigger anger. A lot has to do with the way you view any situation.

Black women's anger or that *Sapphire* behavior is only allowed because it's dysfunctional to black women and other black people, mainly other women and children. If it were hurting anyone who has more power, it would never be tolerated and would have been stamped out long ago. So black women "think" they're exercising power when actually they're being self-destructive, causing others to not want to be around them.

I repeat: The world *does not care* that black women are angry because angry black women don't hurt anyone else but themselves and other black folks around them. I mean, black women don't blow up buildings or countries and never go after those in real power or the predators in their community when they get angry.

I want to post some article links about mammies, sapphires and jezebels, but I haven't done it because it really makes for painful reading. I may do it anyway, so that some of us can see how it all began and how some bw unknowingly still perpetuate it, thinking that it's just natural for a bw to behave that way.

We're not responsible for what happened to us yesterday, but we are responsible for what we do today. Yet, some of us just *keep on* doing dysfunctional stuff because so many misguided black folks think they're "acting black" when they actually are acting against themselves.

Wed Jan 10, 10:54:00 PM EST

Atasha said...

I truly enjoyed reading this post.

> *it's unhealthy and uses up a lot of emotional energy. .*

I cannot tell you how many times I've found myself using these same words, trying to explain this to people. Not sure if it worked.

> *Remember that men are not attracted to angry women—no matter how justifiable your anger may be. Likewise, I, for one, am not attracted to angry men and have always steered clear of them.*

These were my favorite parts of this post. If only people knew how true that was. I feel the same way. One meeting and that was the 1st and last. No one wants to be around someone who's angry regardless of colour.

(I also enjoy reading the comments.)

Wed Jan 10, 10:59:00 PM EST

Halima said...

> *On the social front, it turns many black women into shrewish Sapphires and puts them at a major disadvantage when it comes to relating to men, because while they're being angry at white men and sometimes black men, other women are being friendly towards ALL groups of men—giving these men the green light (as I did for a few minutes with the bank officer). Remember that men are not attracted to angry women—no matter how justifiable your anger may be. Likewise, I, for one, am not attracted to angry men and have always steered clear of them.*

I highlighted this because I think it is so important for women to realise that women as a whole get penalised for being angry and dour-faced.

I used to get angry about the unfairness of it all, but I have now got myself a punching bag, which I use to work off my anger and get back to normal, because trust me, we pay hugely for anything less than a sunny disposition, no matter how justified we are to be angry!

Women get penalised for being serious-faced (I am serious-faced lol), for having an opinion, even for being intelligent, but the one you can and should want to change is being angry!

http://dateawhiteguy.blogspot.com/

Thu Jan 11, 07:35:00 AM EST

Evia said...

> ...women get penalised for being serious-faced (I am serious-faced lol), for having an opinion, even for being intelligent, but the one you can and should want to change is being angry!

Halima, so true! Throughout history, many women, among **all** groups, have been penalized for being intelligent and having an opinion, especially when they are more intelligent than the surrounding men or when their opinion goes against men or those in power.

Regarding anger, my main point is that I'm not saying that black women shouldn't get angry, because their anger is most often righteous. My point is we must focus on managing the anger so that we don't lose anymore than we've already lost and learn to channel that vast amount of emotional energy that they use being angry in a positive direction.

For ex. there are some blogs and forums online where black women spend enormous amounts of energy gnashing their teeth about how black men have 'done bw wrong', and this never ends because you and I realize that for the most part, black men don't care about black women's anger at them. At the end of all of that talking, black women therefore feel worse—even more angry and alone.

Now, I don't have a punching bag. LOL! Instead, I vowed many years ago that I wasn't going to carry around a bunch of stress or allow anyone to keep me feeling bad—that I was going to somehow turn every negative situation that happened to me into a gain, and I've succeeded overwhelmingly with that. That philosophy is very empowering because it allows me to see many problematic situations neutrally. I usually see them as a challenge with an embedded opportunity to learn something. So I don't punch; instead I face and wrestle with these challenges. I've grown tremendously as a result of "wrestling" because even if I don't succeed totally, I always end up farther ahead in one way or another.

So when a situation occurs that triggers my anger, I quickly switch the initial anger response over to challenge mode and I go at it from there. As you may imagine, I'm certainly never bored.

Mind you, there are things that might make me angry, but nothing keeps me angry because remaining angry is a choice. I know that many people don't realize how relatively easy it is to change the circumstances of their lives for the better, (not perfection) given that they have average intelligence and good health, but this is why I keep stressing 'attitude' because attitude drives 90% of your life. People will argue and argue that it's just not that easy, but it mostly depends on how a person views a situation.

This is why I know that if more black women could learn to view situations in their lives differently and change their script, their circumstances would drastically *improve* and many, many more of them could have more fulfilling lives in general.

Thu Jan 11, 09:15:00 AM EST

Anonymous said...

AMEN. It's about time another black woman said this. I'm so happy all black women aren't asleep at the wheel. I too am a very happy black female. I smile, say hello, and the men (all kinds) flock to me.

Thu Jan 11, 09:42:00 AM EST

8

The Loving Case—40th Anniversary—Won Us the Right To Love Who We Choose

June 6, 2007, 6:15 a.m.

—PICTURE : Mildred and Richard Loving

June 12th 2007 marks the 40th anniversary of the "Loving Decision," the landmark Supreme Court ruling that struck down laws in all states against people of different races marrying each other. Anti-miscegenation laws were enacted to prevent blacks and whites from marrying in order to maintain the "purity" of the white race. The Loving Decision, in effect, demolished these state-sponsored apartheid-styled laws in the United States.

Very often, major social advancement is made in a society when a person or persons go against the prevailing norms of that society, and oftentimes they do it simply because the norms just don't make sense to them. The people in this case were a black woman and a white man who were high school sweethearts.

In 1958, this Virginia couple—Mildred and Richard—went to Washington D.C. where interracial marriages were legal and got married. When they returned home to Virginia, where IR marriages were illegal, they were arrested and jailed. After their trial, they were found guilty of violating the anti-miscegenation laws of Virginia and the judge offered them a deal: leave the state for 25 years or go to prison. To avoid this harsh penalty for the "crime" of loving each other openly and desiring to sanction their love with marriage, the Lovings agreed to leave Virginia. They relocated to Washington, D.C. and filed a lawsuit challenging this unjust treatment. Finally, after nine years of numerous court actions, "on June 12, 1967, the nation's highest court voted unanimously to overturn the conviction of Richard and Mildred Loving," and interracial marriages were legalized in all of the states.

The Supreme Court unanimously ruled: "Marriage is one of the 'basic civil rights of man,' fundamental to our very existence and survival. To deny this fundamental freedom on so unsupportable a basis as the racial classifications embodied in these statutes, classifications so directly subversive of the principle of equality at the heart of the Fourteenth Amendment, is surely to deprive all the State's citizens of liberty without due process of law. The Fourteenth Amendment requires that the freedom of choice to marry not be restricted by invidious racial discriminations. Under our Constitution, the freedom to marry, or not to marry, a person of another race resides with the individual and cannot be infringed by the State."

Chief Justice Earl Warren concluded by saying, "These convictions must be reversed. It is so ordered."

When asked why she risked her life to challenge laws against miscegenation, surely one of the pillars of chattel slavery, Mildred said, "It wasn't my doing. It was God's work."

Wow! We owe Mildred Jeter and Richard Loving so much! Darren and I will definitely celebrate Loving Day by doing something special.

I also found it way beyond ironic that though Mildred Jeter was a black woman, bw—in 2007—are the least likely group of American women to take advantage of interracial love and marriage opportunities. The *black community* embraced and trumpeted every other victory that was won during the civil rights struggle except for this one. If you don't know why, then I know you were born last night. LOL! Does this spell sexism or does this spell sexism?

Black women, let me repeat this again, you have the right to love anyone you choose of any skin shade or background. AA women have, in effect, been taught or *indoctrinated* by the black collective to give up this right. You've been taught that it is wrong or 'disloyal' to love any man other than a black man. This is why some of you are still struggling with guilt about even wanting to love a white or other non-black man. This is why some of you are scared to even voice the desire to date, love, or sex a white man or even be attracted to one. This is why a woman I know felt she had to travel 50 miles out of her town to date a wm—because she was afraid to be seen with him in her town. The way she talked about it, you would have thought he was a known pedophile! LOL!

Many non-black people and, especially non-Americans cannot understand why it is that so many bm, ww, aw, hw, hm, etc. embrace and act on this most basic right and increasingly date others from other races and backgrounds without an afterthought, whereas AA women are seen as having hang-ups about *dating out*.

Black women, don't deny it. Many of you do have hang-ups about "dating out" as we can clearly see from the thousands of comments here and all of the angst expressed here. You've got to talk about this more and more and do so openly so that other bw around you can feel free to think it, talk about it, and act on this most basic right. We must bring it out in the open and talk about it as *normal* in order for it to be normalized. This will help many bw to work through their hang-ups that could prevent them from finding suitable and loving mates.

Some bw's hang-ups are so complex and multi-layered until many of you project your hang-ups onto to wm and other men and declare that they don't want you or think that they don't find you attractive or only want you for sex. Some of you don't realize it, but many of you who are strongly attracted to wm create these *blocks* to shield yourself from taking a chance at love with a wm. You're simply afraid of community disapproval. Likewise, some white men also create similar blocks to protect themselves from taking a chance on love with a bw which they fear will invite parental and/or white community disapproval.

Back to bw: Black women, these are merely your projections in many cases. These are illusions that some of you have created to ease your guilt and fears about wanting to date white and other white-skinned men. These illusions help you to remain more comfortable about staying in your box. These illusions also are among the reasons why you don't just turn your back on DBR-bm. The bulk of bw in the U.S., for sure, have been strongly conditioned to remain loyal to bm even though there is virtually *no* reciprocity.

African American women are forever being put through an ever-churning indoctrination machine. I hear the churning every time I mingle with black women and the topic of men comes up, or as one commenter here calls it: "the conversation about bm." You will note that so many African American women simply can't take their focus off AA men. It even happens here on an interracial marriage blog when black women go and bring tidbits of that "conversation" here from poisonous, anti-bw blogs and boards where damaged-beyond-repair bm spout their disdain for bw.

Logically or in normal circumstances, any sensible woman would not have any problem turning her back instantly on a DBR man, especially when there are other quality men in the surroundings. This is why many other people absolutely cannot understand why so many bw continue to even think about or get involved with DBR men.

When I talk with African women sometimes, they question this phenomenon. They cannot understand this at all, particularly because these DBR men are frequently womanizers and don't financially or emotionally support their children. Many times, African women have asked me, "Why do you bw here let those useless men come near you?"

Black women, this lowers us in the eyes of *some* other people in the global village. Some people question whether we have normal intelligence. Even many DBR-bm are now castigating bw for having multiple out-of-wedlock children and even laughing at bw for being *babymamas* when some of these same men are often *babydaddies*. In other words, they laugh and heap ridicule on some of you who have opened your legs to them and allowed them to plant their seed, which they then abandon.

My blog has shown through numerous pictures that there are many loving and loveable men of other races who are in loving relationships with bw who look just like you. I've also shown that the type of wm—who is attracted to bw—usually has a much wider appreciation for the full spectrum of black female beauty than a typical bm. Many other men, aside from white men, also appreciate the beauty of black females.

We have beautiful bodies when layers of excess fat do not hide our curves and distort our skin. Medical professionals have pointed out that, in general, black women's skin and bodies age better than any other group of women IF we take care of ourselves. Other men also notice our spirit, that pizzaz/sassiness, etc., and some of them adore that about us. However, no one likes the anger or the nasty attitude of the shrill Sapphire types.

Make this day—Day 1, that you make the effort to learn to value yourself. Refuse to believe any of the poisonous hype that's spewed at you from anyone who doesn't recognize your value. Stay away from venomous people and things that spray poison on you to weaken you and make you doubt yourself. This is all very deliberate—a part of the machine to keep black women caged and exploited by bm and the bc that do virtually nothing to reciprocate or actually address your womanly needs for genuine love and fulfillment.

Last, but definitely not least, is that you must be determined to get rid of excess weight. Too many AA women are carrying an unattractive and unhealthy amount of weight around. Let's not mince words here. I've noticed that some people refer to themselves as having a "few extra pounds" or "thick." But is it just a *few extra pounds*? As more and more bw die and/or are debilitated from weight-related illnesses, everyone—even those who say they love you—seems to be afraid to tell you that the weight is *very* excessive in some cases. Added to that, many of you have been bamboozled by the black community into thinking that it's okay or normal for bw to carry around excess weight, with ridiculous statements like: "Only a dog wants a bone."

This is a lie. Excess weight and obesity are *not* normal. Just because others in your family or environment are overweight does not mean it's a normal situation. Many situations in a typical AA person's environment are not normal. My grandmother was very overweight, got diabetes, and lost parts of her body as a result, before she died too soon. This was not normal, yet I continue to hear black folks telling bw that we can carry more weight. Enough!

And please don't find consolation in the fact that lots of white and other women are also fat. You don't have to deal with their heart attacks, strokes or diabetes, but you will have to deal with yours. On the dating front, I think my head is just going to roll off if I hear another black woman say, "but white women and other women are overweight too and bm still want them!" Who cares? You shouldn't. You shouldn't even care who DBRbm want because you shouldn't even be thinking about them. Think about whom and what you want (unless you want a DBRbm) because the more you think about a thing, you increase the likelihood that you will get it.

Stop using other *excuses* to remain excessively overweight such as it's your 'thyroid,' your 'metabolism,' or the 'medicine' you're taking. No one believes that. That insults peoples' intelligence. LOL!

Many of us have put on too much weight at some point in our lives. Aside from a relatively small number of people, overweight is due to 'excess caloric intake' and not enough physical activity to burn off those calories. If you consume more calories than you burn off, you will gain weight. Reduce your caloric intake and get into a regular fitness routine. However, even if you are slim, you still need a regular fitness routine to maintain and/or improve your body's functioning.

Hmmmm, after standing on that soapbox spouting off, I think it's time for me to get over to the gym.

Posted by Evia at 6/06/2007 06:45:00 AM

9

Do White Men "Step Up" to Black Women?

January 23, 2007, 5:00 p.m.

• PICTURE Link: Lewis (Scooter) Libby and Harriet Grant
Lewis "Scooter" Libby (Vice Pres. Dick Cheney's former chief of staff and Asst. to Dick Cheney for National Security Affairs) and wife, Harriet Grant (former staff lawyer of the Senate Judiciary Committee)

• PICTURE: Mellody Hobson and Chris Albrecht (scroll down)
Mellody Hobson, President of Ariel Mutual Funds & Chris Albrecht, CEO and Chairman of HBO

• PICTURE: Prince Albert (of Monaco) and Nicole Coste
• Article and Picture: Prince Albert (of Monaco) and Nicole Coste & Son (Picture & Article)

Some white men are definitely "stepping up! " These are power couples. Mellody Hobson is the President of Ariel Capital Management, LLC, one of the largest African American-owned money management and mutual fund companies in the country and a regular financial advice contributor on ABC's "Good Morning America."

I don't know how many of you may have watched last night's episode of the new TV series "Lincoln Heights" on the ABC Family Channel about a black cop who has moved his family (wife and 3 kids) back to the tough neighborhood of 'Lincoln Heights' where he grew up.

The series has a storyline about a budding IR relationship between the 17 year old daughter "Cassie" and a white classmate, "Charles." You can Google this series. I heard or read somewhere that the executive producer of this series is a black woman, a graduate of Spellman,.

In this episode, it's very obvious that Charles really likes Cassie and she likes him too, but she's waiting for him to say something definite. Anyway, the mother asked Cassie during last night's episode how the relationship with Charles is going and Cassie complains that Charles won't "step up." Later in the episode, Charles has had a couple of beers and he begins to profess his real feelings for Cassie and she asks him whether it's the beer talking or whether it's how he really feels. He swears it's how he really feels, but she cuts him off and tells him, and I paraphrase, "Tell me tomorrow when the beer is out of your system."

This is exactly what we were talking about a couple of weeks ago here, how sometimes white men won't directly express their interest in a black woman in the same way black women are accustomed to black men "stepping up" to let a woman know for sure that he's interested. On the other hand, I've read where some white men say that white women won't tell a man how she really feels either, so is this a more general cultural trait among whites? I dunno.

During my dating years—if a man I liked made it his business to be around me as much as possible, or showed in some other way that he was interested as Charles does with Cassie, I always helped him to express it. I'd ask him flirtatiously, "Are you always hanging around me because you like me or is it because I'm totally irresistible?" or something to that effect. Of course, what man is not going to say "yes" to both? LOL!

Sometimes, a beer or a glass of wine does loosen him up. I realize that some women like a man to be more aggressive, because they feel that if he's too timid to ask her out, he'll also be timid in the—ahem, "other departments." In my experience, this was never the case, at all! Sometimes, a lot of the posturing and cool 'swagger" that some men have is just a front, whereas, some of the most timid-acting men are, well, insatiable stallions in other 'departments!' LOL!

The point is that sometimes, the woman can help to break the ice.

To White/Non-Black Men:

I don't know how many unattached white/non-bm men read my blog because all of the ones who e-mail me privately or comment here are already married to or dating a black woman, but in case some of you guys are still looking, I'm asking some of the women here to mention specifically how you can best approach them, for best results: the "dos and don'ts." Naturally, all black women are different, but at least you'll have some guidelines.

Posted by Evia at 1/23/2007 05:02:00 PM

COMMENTS:
Anonymous said...

I'm happily married now but when it comes to advice? Let's see. Well, I'd have to say if you're a white male interested in a black woman, do not automatically presume that she's interested in the so called "*wigger*" (Vanilla Ice, Eminem, etc...) type. There are plenty of women of color who prefer and are only attracted to the straight laced, "Wonderbread", computer "geek", white-collar professional types. Basically, you don't have to be "down" or pretend to be. On the contrary, it's best to *always* be yourself

Also, treat a black woman the same way you'd treat a white, Asian, Hispanic or other woman. We're not a different species, after all. We're just human beings with the same desires, strengths, and fragilities as any other woman. And don't give up. When you do get out there in the IR dating world, if you have a few bad experiences with black women, don't feel that they're representative of *all* women of color. Keep the faith and get out there again. Relationships usually end for good reasons, so don't live in the past, or grow bitter. Move on and continue to be open because it's a big world out there full of growing numbers of women of color the world over who are just like you. Open up and be willing to experience love, which is a true blessing when you're fortunate enough to find it without racial restraints. Good luck to all!

Wed Jan 24, 12:10:00 PM EST

Zabeth said...

A couple of things:

1. I think it's a mistake to assume that a WM is going to "step" to you the same way that at BM will. Yes we're all human, we all live in the same country, but we're all going to operate differently.

2. I too would be leery of a man who only wanted to profess his interest in me after a few drinks; any woman would.

3. For WM, I think the best way is just to approach her, just start talking to her. I realize some women can be cold and unreceptive and that can be a put-off. But I think the best way is to identify women who seem to be approachable and appear to be comfortable around "mixed company."

4. Some women assume that a timid guy will not only be timid in the bedroom, but in life. I don't want a guy I can walk all over. But Evia is right about the swagger thing; often, it's just a front.

5. Coaching it out of a guy can be helpful too. BW may take this personally as in, "if he really was interested in me he'd come out and say it." Well remember, he may have this same difficulty with white, Hispanic, and Asian women.

Wed Jan 24, 01:59:00 PM EST

Evia said...

> Well, I'd have to say if you're a white male interested in a black woman, do not automatically presume that she's interested in the so called "wigger" (Vanilla Ice, Eminem, etc...) type.

Thanks, Anonymous, for this response. I think this is super advice. I certainly never appreciate it when white people try to "act black" or think that they have to act "cool" or "down" in order for me to be comfortable around them. I remember one of my male in-laws said to me that I must get very bored when I'm in the midst of a bunch of the white in-laws at family gatherings and such. I had to think on that one. Was he saying that black folks are never boring to be around or what? I still haven't figured that one out. LOL!

My husband definitely never tried to "act black." I would have blown him off if he had. I'm not even attracted to black men who try to "act black"—walking with that swagger and all and trying to "talk black." Dr. King was a master of the English language. Why wasn't he *black* enough to emulate? It's unnatural for all the males of any group to walk with a swagger, that rocking walk. I've seen young black boys practice walking like that because they think that they're not an authentic AA male until they can master that walk! My ex-husband, a continental African, asked me once why it is that so many AA males walk the same way? I tried to explain why they "affect" that rocking walk, but he didn't ever understand what the connection was between that 'rocking' walk and being black or of African descent. SMH

Wed Jan 24, 02:04:00 PM EST

Danny said...

Great blog post! I am an unattached white man who has dated a number of black women in the past. I hate to say it, but I think the Cassie/Charles dynamic you refer to has been evident with me in past relationships. But you know, it has worked out well. I think publicly shy and publicly aggressive can go well together, as long as they're equals in private. That's what I strive for!

Also, I love that show! I bet "Cassie and Charles" will be one of those TV relationships everybody talks about soon.

Wed Jan 24, 06:21:00 PM EST

Evia said...

Danny, Welcome! Thanks for your comments.

My husband, Darren, is more of the intellectual type, so he's not the outwardly aggressive, macho-man type, at all. He's low-keyed, soft-spoken, but very sharp. He is aggressive enough for me and more important: "effective," in all the ways that really count. Privately? Well, I'll just say I have no complaints. Whew!

I've always been attracted to brainy, savvy men. It never mattered to me whether they were publicly aggressive or low-keyed. About the low-keyed thing, if you've got it going on, you don't need to flaunt it. But for me personally, he has to have the intellect to get out of a paper bag all by himself, so to speak.

There are many black women out there who are attracted to white men like you. As someone said above, don't take it personally if you approach a black woman in a respectful way and she blows you off. Don't even think about it. Just go on to the next bw, if black women are your choice.

Yeah, I really like "Lincoln Heights" too. Charles and Cassie will get together—after a few more hurdles, of course! LOL!

Wed Jan 24, 06:54:00 PM EST

Gatamala said...

Evia - this is off topic but I can't email from work.

Another couple: Scooter Libby & Harriet Grant

Ha-ha, I guess we take the bad with the good!

Also: Robin Givens & Mark Schenkenberg! She used to date Brad Pitt before you know who scared him off.

Thu Jan 25, 10:38:00 AM EST

Meli said...

Viggo Mortensen of (Lord of the Rings trilogy) fame among other great films, used to date (in 2003-4) a Black British star, Josie D'Arby. I can't find pics of them together, but her pics are on IMDB, the movie data base. US weekly magazine pictured them together at that time.

Thu Jan 25, 01:08:00 PM EST

Meli said...

Is Harriet Grant a Black woman? I have "googled" her and nothing comes up relating to African American interests or the like.

Thu Jan 25, 01:29:00 PM EST

Evia said...

Gatamala, I did pull up a picture of Harriet Grant and Scooter Libby, but from the angle of the picture, I can't determine whether she's black. Do you have a better picture? If so, please send to my e-mailbox. Tks.

Thu Jan 25, 04:28:00 PM EST

Anonymous said...

Just a small correction: Prince Albert and Nicole Coste are no longer together. She is the mother of his son, but they are not a couple anymore.

Thu Jan 25, 07:20:00 PM EST

Evia said...

> Just a small correction: Prince Albert and Nicole Coste are no longer together. She is the mother of his son, but they are not a couple anymore.

Thank you, Anonymous, however, I realize that some of these

relationships may no longer exist, however they did exist at one point which shows the attraction between the two involved. Same race relationships don't last either—sometimes.

In case anyone is wondering why I've posted the gallery of bf-wm couples in the sidebar, I've done it to prove two *very* significant points about bf-wm relationships, in particular.

#1 There are *many* bf-wm relationships these days comprised of people ranging from the very prominent and high-profile people to the very ordinary folks, like your neighbors and me and my husband. These pictures and related articles are necessary as proof of these relationships because so many black women, as indicated by some comments here, still believe and argue vehemently that white men are interested in black women only for sex. This is *not* true, as the many pics of bw-wm married couples and those in long-term relationships prove. Whereas this was totally true at one time, this is fear mongering and a stereotype now. The gallery of pictures shows beyond any doubt that a cross-section of white men date, marry, and have families with black women.

#2 Also, these pictures prove that many white men who date and marry bw are able to appreciate a wide range of black female beauty—from the very dark-skinned black woman to the very light skinned ones. This proof is necessary because many black women and many other folks still believe that white men who date bw are only or mostly interested in light-skinned bw who have European features and hair, unambiguous features, or so-called non-West African features. Not true.

Thu Jan 25, 07:52:00 PM EST
Mel [not Meli] **said...**

Evia! First, great blog! I'm an AA female, currently unattached (for a bit too long now), and I've never dated a non-Black man, but your blog, while I don't agree with all opinions expressed, gives me and others a lot of food for thought. I appreciate your chutzpah to put this together. It's time that we control our own P.R., because if we don't do it, no one else will.

And, it's time for the white guys to "step up." There are many that seem to be scared or too comfortable admiring us from afar. But on the other hand, do we really want guys who can't step up to the plate even to say "hello"?

Anyway, my question is about the Mellody Hobson picture (as well as pictures of the other couples). How do we know that these are (or were) bona fide couples? Some are obvious and known in our society, and some we get to learn are couples from the text under the picture, etc. But, the Mellody Hobson picture (in particular) has no such text. So how do we know that she is actually *dating* this guy? Or did you put the picture up as another example of a BW and a WM who are powerful, moneyed, and who are not afraid to appear in public together?

Thanks! Great blog!

Fri Jan 26, 04:21:00 PM EST

Ann said...

Beautiful article!

Regarding your pic of Deneice Graves (in your sidebar): she is the bomb! I love her fortitude and resilience, and especially this quote from the article you linked:

> But, I really am of the belief system that you work as hard as you can and make it impossible for them to say no.

Ms. Graves is a woman who has truly paid her dues, a woman who believes in "lifting" as she climbs. A woman sublime.

And opera!

Anyone who does not love opera, well...they just do not know what they are missing. Not to mention, that "Carmen" is my favorite opera, especially the *"Habanera" aria:

> L'amour est un oiseau rebelle [Love is a rebellious bird]
> que nul ne peut apprivoiser,   [that cannot be tamed]
> et c'est bien en vain qu'on l'appelle, [and you can call him quite in vain]
> s'il lui convient de refuser. [if it suits him not to come]
> Rien n'y fait, menace ou prière, [nothing helps, neither threats nor prayer]
> l'un parle bien, l'autre se tait:

Et c'est l'autre que je préfère,
Il n'a rien dit mais il me plaît.
L'amour! l'amour! l'amour! l'amour!
L'amour est enfant de Bohême,
il n'a jamais, jamais connu de loi;
si tu ne m'aimes pas, je t'aime:
si je t'aime, prends garde à toi! etc.
L'oiseau que tu croyais surprendre
battit de l'aile et s'envola ...
l'amour est loin, tu peux l'attendre;
tu ne l'attends plus, il est là!
Tout autour de toi, vite, vite,
il vient, s'en va, puis il revient ...
tu crois le tenir, il t'évite,
tu crois l'éviter, il te tient.
L'amour! l'amour!, lamour, l'amour!
[Ole! Viva la Diva!

[*Note: You can Google the entire translation of this opera.]
Fri Jan 26, 06:14:00 PM EST

Clarice said...

Most men will not approach a woman unless there is some interest, and if a man thinks he's going to get shot down he is not going to approach. So it is unlikely that the approach is going to be a total "cold call." There has to reasonably be some sign, no matter how small, of openness or receptiveness. So, remember BW are women, first and foremost.

BW are not a different species, so the best approach is the same that would work with anyone. Treat a BW like any other woman or any other person. In short "come correct or do not come at all" i.e. with dignity, respect, courtesy and consideration. DO: Be yourself. DO: Act with dignity, respect, courtesy and consideration.

BW who are open to IRs tend to be, as a general rule, independent and open minded and are quietly effective at living on their own terms and making their way. They are typically comfortable with who they are and what they believe with quiet conviction—"to thine own self be true." In light of that, this type of BW is unlikely to want drama and/or flamboyance at least not initially. These BW who are looking for serious (i.e. more than just a good time) relationships (IR or not) want a good man who treats them with kindness and respect, is inclusive and considerate with morals and wants to do the right thing. This type of man is generally comfortable in who he is, respects himself and his choices and treats others the same way. That said, these BW may tend to be a bit reserved but polite until they get a feel for the situation.

Women, but especially BW, are expected to play so many roles that until the woman has an idea of what the situation or circumstance requires, she may hold back to see what evolves. 'Waiting to exhale' as it were, until they see that they will be respected and accepted for themselves, where they are.

BW want what anyone wants: to be respected treated with dignity, courtesy and an acceptance of differences. A guy who approaches with respect, honesty, and sincerity and is clear and direct in his intent, but never rude, crude or uncouth, has a chance. If you want to ask her out, simply just ask. DO: Take a deep breath, relax and ask. As a semi-geeky tech sort of BW, my tendency is to be a bit reserved until more information is forthcoming. Computer "geek", white collar professional types are quietly attractive because still waters run deep, but it would be a mistake to write off shyness as "timid."

Gems do not have to advertise. If you are nervous, say so up front; that kind of honesty can be refreshing. It says you are human and you are honest and respect her enough not to try and fake it. That kind of self-disclosure and honest acceptance of self sends a signal that it is safe to exhale.

If a woman turns down a polite request, respond the way you would want someone to treat you if you made a reasonable request that was turned down. Most often, a "no" is not about the recipient; it comes from where the respondent is at that point in time. It's about the respondent's state of mind not the state of the requestor. It is not about you. Chances are a woman who wants a serious relationship has had some home training and it shows, so she may turn you down politely. If not, just remember it is not about you and move on. Hope this helps Dan and others.

Fri Jan 26, 07:40:00 PM EST
Eleanor said...

Evia, Ann, Chr and Meli: Ladies, this is Eleanor from Canada. Just want you to be the first to know that my husband got the job in

Charleston, SC! He is still there...returning tomorrow with loads of pics and exciting news to share! Thanks for all your words of encouragement. You rock!

Fri Jan 26, 07:45:00 PM EST

Ann said...

Eleanor, congratulations! I hope you and your husband have a wonderful, long life together, and that his job is truly rewarding for him. I've only seen pictures of Charleston, but, I'm sure (no, I know) that you will enjoy living in this beautiful city. Welcome to the South, dear Sister, and may God send all His Blessings to you and your husband.

Peace.

Fri Jan 26, 07:54:00 PM EST

Meli said...

That is most excellent news Eleanor! My sentiments are exactly as Ann's...Welcome to the South. I am happy for you and your husband!

Fri Jan 26, 10:48:00 PM EST

Evia said...

Happy to hear the good news, Eleanor! I know that you, a Canadian, were a bit nervous about living down South with a white husband, but I'm sure all will be fine.

Sat Jan 27, 09:24:00 AM EST

Chr said...

Eleanor - Congrats! Now I have an excuse to visit Charleston.

Sat Jan 27, 03:33:00 PM EST

Eleanor said...

Ann, Evia, Char, Meli...Ladies it would be wonderful to have a "meet and greet" in Charleston with you all. Wouldn't that be something! OMG...then I (Madame Canadian) could be your tour guide. How hilarious would that be...having some newly arrived immigrant showing you around your *own* country/state! Ok, ok, I'm getting carried away with the tour guide thing, but seriously speaking, hubby and I would welcome you all there!

Evia dear, I apologize for temporarily taking this blog off topic...but I just wanted to update you and thought it best to do so at the bottom of this current article. Sorry everyone for interrupting the flow of responses to this article. Greaaat article by the way...as usual!

Sat Jan 27, 06:19:00 PM EST
Ann said...
Evia, not meaning to get off topic, but, for those of you who are "60 Minutes" fans, there will be an episode covering Bestbuy's "Geek Squad." Unless some trivial football game runs over into the time slot, everyone should be able to see it, except I am not sure of those living on the West Coast.

Anyway, as I am sure as all of you know, I have a very definite weakness for the "geeks."

Eleanor, Congrats!! Now I have an excuse to visit Charleston.

I second that, Char!
Come to think of it, I do have a vacation coming up in February, but...No. Best to let you two get settled in, get used to your new surroundings, and allow your husband time to ease into his new job. Just try and keep in touch with us, letting us all know how you are both doing.

You are both in all our prayers. Peace.

Sat Jan 27, 09:37:00 PM EST
Meli said...
Eleanor, that is awful sweet of you. I plan a visit there this summer because I missed it on my November trip. It would be nice to have some sort of a meeting like once a year for the members on this site, kind of like a book club or discussion group of sorts. Charleston can be our first little convention! I am jumping the gun too Eleanor. LOL!

The Pemberley Book Club comes to mind since you mentioned that. I am a Jane Austen fan; "Pride and Prejudice" is my favorite book and I never knew that there was such a following, but once a year a group of women who also love "Pride and Prejudice" meet to discuss the book and the author—how neat!

Once you and your husband settle in well to Charleston, SC, you will be happy there I am sure of it.

Sun Jan 28, 12:01:00 AM EST
Meli said...
Ann...I hope that you find your cute geek-type fellow. Those guys are so very smart and unassuming, which makes them quite attrac-

tive. Men with brain power are so amazing.

Sun Jan 28, 12:12:00 AM EST

Chr said...

I too have a weakness for a smart man. That is one of the qualities I love about my husband. I was hooked after our first date.

Sun Jan 28, 08:13:00 AM EST

Clarice said...

A smart man is definitely sweet. I can't wait for 60 Minutes tonight.

Sun Jan 28, 04:27:00 PM EST

Ann said...

Just caught the "60 Minutes" "Get Me a Geek!" broadcast and it was great!

On a different note: the American Korean War deserter. Interesting. And as an added input, he was married to the daughter of a Korean woman and a black diplomat, and had a child with her. (She was his 2nd wife, wife No. 1 having died some years ago.)

But, anyway, back to the geeks.

Geeks definitely rule: who ya gonna call when your computer goes on the fritz! Geek Squad to the rescue.

In my case, I am still capable of setting up my video/audio systems without having to call tech support. I'm even able to hook up two vcrs together, hook up an LD player, or CED player to each component, still able to audio dub and tape (well, I still have my old Sony SL-5600 Betamax), and that's one feature that I miss on these new-fangled vcrs. Audio dubbing.

Another thing: during the episode, one of the geeks asked the reporter to quickly find the "volume" buttons on his remote control. I decided to play along.

I found mine immediately, while the reporter was still looking for the volume control. (Hint: maybe it's just me, but I'd say if you are looking for the volume buttons, *always* look to the lower *right area*, *upper right* area, or *lower left* area, depending on the manufacturer. Seems like those areas are where the volume buttons are located on many remotes, be they DVD, TV, or most audio/video universal remotes. Although in the rare case, the volume button is located right square *in the middle* of the remote.)

Another thing that I noticed is that many of the geeks had a good sense of humor. Definitely a plus for any person. Plus it came as no surprise to me that the geeks came off as "human", and not as stiff as some people may assume they are.

Some people say that geeks are rude, egotistical, and insensitive, but, I have *yet* to encounter a rude geek who helps me out with computer tech support when I need it, whenever my computer gives me problems. And I'm sure many geeks are laughing all the way to the dating market since some people are finally waking up to the true beauty of geeks.

I prefer to say that they have been quietly plodding along, honing their skills and craft while becoming very alluring, very sexy, and very desirable.

Sun Jan 28, 08:38:00 PM EST
Evia said...
Mel, Welcome. Thanks for the kudos and the comments.

> *I'm an AA female, currently unattached (for a bit too long now) and I've never dated a non-Black man, but your blog, while I don't agree with all opinions expressed, gives me and others a LOT of food for thought. I appreciate your chutzpah. . .*

Well thanks, Mel, not to get you confused with "Meli," but actually I don't think of it as having chutzpah at all. If black women are in search of a loving relationship, it's just common sense to me to look at where the bulk of the men are who are most likely to be suitable.

In the USA, white men are the largest group of males who are most compatible culturally with AA females of a certain demographic/class, and white men are still marrying at a quite high rate. African American women have been indoctrinated to mate with black males, but these women can, and IMO, *should* increase their relationships pool and mate with and marry *any* compatible, loving and lovable, interested man. At a time when a very large chunk of AA males are out of the marriage market altogether (engaged in nefarious activities, not attending or college or vocational school, in prison, emotionally unsuitable, etc.), or deciding deliberately not to get married, or are out-marrying, it's just common sense and a viable route for many AA females to date and marry white males and other non-black males, IF we're being realistic. It's not as if we're biologically unable to mate with non-AA men. I know I'm not!

Some people are advocating that AA females move to Africa or another black country to find black men, however, that's not feasible for most AA women. So, that's ridiculous for black women to hold out for that! However, relationships with compatible black men from other cultures is an option that should be explored also, if it's feasible.

I dated my share of men from various cultures because I've always been very interested in people of other cultures. I married one of those men the first time around. The cultural differences can be and usually are a major issue in intercultural relationships for some people and can be very difficult to manage because people are usually a product of their culture, much more so than their race.

> *It's time that we control our own PR, because if we don't do it, no one else will.*

It certainly *is* time for us to be proactive about our PR. Negativity abounds about AA women and for the most part, we're just silently taking all of these punches that, in the last decade or so, have come mainly from AA men.

I'm totally unapologetic when I assert the AA woman's *right* to do whatever she needs to do to secure a long-term loving relationship with a loveable man—whatever his race or background. No AA woman needs to be alone—*if* she wants a quality mate. That can be disastrous to her emotional health. Poor emotional health often causes physical health problems. No AA woman should feel she should sacrifice herself for the community by remaining single or searching forever for a suitable black man when there are numerous men from other backgrounds available to her in the here and now.

As it stands now, many young, attractive, hardworking AA women are married to work, community, and church. White men are the *largest* group of "other" men available to any AA woman—no matter how this issue is crunched. Is it common sense to overlook the largest group of males in the environment or remain unreceptive to them *if* you desire a mate?

> *And, it's time for the white guys to step up. There are many that seem to be scared or too comfortable admiring us from afar.*

The way I see it is that white men operate differently from black men in this regard. We've discussed that here to an extent. In addition, there is so much PC operating in the black-white social arena that impacts the behavior on both sides, sometimes in unnatural ways!

> But on the other hand, do we really want guys who can't step up to the plate even to say "hello?"

Well, as I've said, my husband is far from being the chest-beating, macho-man type of man. I can't stand that type of man from any background. Darren is laid back, soft-spoken, and much more of the intellectual type. Some women may have thought he couldn't "step up," but I'm glad I didn't look at him in that way. I prefer a man who relies on his brain to protect and provide for his family, and he's done that very well and "steps up" with the best of them in other areas. LOL!

> Anyway, my question is about the Mellody Hobson picture (as well as pictures of the other couples). How do we know that these are (or were) bona fide couples? Some are obvious and known in our society, and some we get to learn are couples from the text under the picture, etc. But, the Mellody Hobson picture (in particular) has no such text. So how do we know that she is actually dating this guy??

It's beyond interesting that no matter how much proof is provided, some people will still doubt whether a wm and a bw are a "couple." I think this question reflects the seriously negative state of race relations in the U.S. I don't believe this question of "are they really together" would continue to come up in any other country.

Actually, I have no way of proving that anyone is married or dating—even if I were posting same-race couples. I get pictures and information sent to me, culled from the internet and anyone can put anything on the internet. As you know, some people (even of the same race) who claim to be married are not married at all and some who are married or dating will lie about their marriage or relationship for various reasons. The only bf-wm couple who I could prove is actually a "couple" is my husband and me because I have the marriage certificate. LOL! This is not aimed at you, but why is it that a bm-ww couple doesn't need to "prove" they're a couple?

> *Or did you put the picture up as another example of a BW and a WM who are powerful, moneyed, and who are not afraid to appear in public together?*

These 2 people are out together socially, but you may be onto something. *sarcasm* They may both be closet homosexuals and are simply *covering* for each other. Stranger things have occurred.
Sun Jan 28, 09:14:00 PM EST
Felicia said...

> *White men are the largest group of males who are most compatible culturally with AA females of a certain demographic/class.*
>
> *I'm totally unapologetic when I assert the AA woman's right to do whatever she needs to do to secure a long-term loving relationship with a loveable man—whatever his race or background.*
>
> *No AA woman should feel she should remain alone or sacrifice herself for the community by searching forever for a suitable black man when there are numerous men from other backgrounds available to her.*

Talking about the truth, the whole truth, and nothing but the truth. I most definitely concur with your analysis of the situation, Evia. Your train of thought is simple, logical, and empowering. The only women (and men obviously) who are threatened by your clear thinking and open discussion of this very taboo subject matter are those who have foolishly designated themselves the "gatekeepers" of the "community's" public image. What did Bill Cosby say a while back? Actually, not long ago. *"Your dirty laundry gets out of school at 2:30 everyday..."* He, of course, was talking about in this case foul acting black youngsters cuttin' up in the public eye. Maybe some gatekeepers in the community didn't get the memo, but basically, *everybody* (i.e. white folks and other non-blacks) already knows about the often—*not* always but often— sorry state of black relationships and communication between the sexes. Psst! Word is *out* and it's been out for some time now.

Nothing said in this blog is earth-shattering news to anybody! LOL! What's frightening, dangerous, stress-provoking and treasonous to some—make that *most* folks—is the whole unadulterated *truth* is being told. And it's un-sugarcoated (you openly discuss the taboo issue of colorism and don't portray black males as the helpless psychological victims of white men), which makes it unpalatable to the masses.

My feeling is, only 'the truth will set you free.' Black American women need to start limiting themselves to marriage-minded, lovable, undamaged, gainfully employed, non-colorist men regardless of race and nationality who are capable of loving them in return.

It's as simple as that. If that's "controversial" so be it.

> *I prefer a man who relies on his brain to protect and provide for his family and he's done that very well and "steps up" with the best of them in other areas. LOL!*

Girl, tell me about it! You described my husband to a tee. Although you'll continue to attract some detractors to your blog, you're also opening a lot of eyes. More than I think you'll ever know. Keep up the good work!

Mon Jan 29, 12:42:00 PM EST

Tandy said...

E, great blog—love reading it.

I agree with your assessment of the situation, though I'm not AA (Jamaican). I've seen some blogs where BW are constantly bemoaning the plight of the black man, yet they adamantly refuse to look across the racial barriers. I do understand that an IR relationship is not for everyone, but my point is this, what can it hurt to look?

I started looking when I realised that my tastes were no longer compatible with the men I knew and as I moved in search of compatibility, I found white men were more to my liking. I'm just saying: take a chance.

And as for the approach, being yourself, polite, and courteous are good openers.

Mon Jan 29, 02:38:00 PM EST
Meli said...

Felicia, I am high-fiving you in cyber space. Your comment was just right on target. That "dirty laundry" comment made by Bill Cosby was so profound, sad, and painfully true all rolled in one. You are right. People know...people know!

Mon Jan 29, 03:14:00 PM EST
Las said...

> *Although you'll continue to attract some detractors to your blog, you're also opening a lot of eyes.*

Reading that statement I just want to ask, Evia, have you ever had any "detractors" to your blog? I ask this because from the time you started this blog, I don't really recall any "detractors" per se. News to me, or maybe I missed something. Maybe you get them privately? Or that statement was meant for future-tense purposes.

With the risk of giving the wrong impression or being accused of something, I just want to say, I know I have opposed some of the things (statistics) that were said on this blog in regards to white men equally being receptive to black women. However, I always encourage black women to not limit themselves to just black men. Other women have said similar and I still got the impression they too want to see more BW with WM, etc. So I am just saying, I'm hoping that none of your readers actually think there are "detractors" posting on this blog, at least not from black women. People have a right to share their respectful opinions. At the end of the day, we all want the same thing, more interested WM with interested BW. We are just sharing different opinions and insight to assist in getting there. Don't mean to cause any conflict, just wanted to share my thoughts.

Mon Jan 29, 05:33:00 PM EST
Evia said...

> *So I am just saying, I'm hoping that none of your readers actually think there are "detractors"*

Yes, Las, I definitely have my detractors and I've spoken about them from time to time on here. I've gotten a few rabid e-mails from black people. Black women are the backbone of the black community.

People know that. I know that, but it's too high of a price to pay to ask a bw to give, give, give and not get what she needs in return. Here's the deal: if you keep giving and never *getting*, you're going to end up empty-handed. Simple arithmetic.

Black women are worn out, emotionally debilitated, not taking care of themselves physically, emotionally or spiritually (I'm not talking about organized religion) and dying like flies as a result, and at young ages. Folks that I know just keep telling black women to keep praying for a good man. I believe in the power of prayer, but I believe that God helps those who help themselves. That's what I was always taught.

Mon Jan 29, 05:46:00 PM EST
Zabeth said...

> Black women are the backbone of the black community. People know that. I know that, but it's too high of a price to pay to ask a bw to give, give, give and not get what she needs in return.

Amen to that. That statement made me think of one of your previous blogs about Mammies, Sapphires, and Jezebels. After reading that particular entry, I began to see a lot of "mammy" in me (and coincidently in my mother as well—that's probably where I learned it). I realized that I was giving way too much of myself and getting very little back in return. So now, I've become more focused on putting my needs and my happiness first.

BTW, this is kind of off topic but still very related. It has been simmering in the tabloid media that P-Diddy has been spotted spending a lot of cozy time with actress Sienna Miller, while Kim Porter, his current girlfriend (not wife) and mother of 3 of his five children (who by the way has just given birth to a set of twin girls) sits back at home. I know that is kind of off topic but this really burns me. Why are so many BW willing to settle for this kind of treatment? If we truly are the backbone of the community, then why don't we value ourselves enough to demand better?

Mon Jan 29, 07:04:00 PM EST
Meli said...

That "back bone" role makes me feel a sense of sadness, neglect, and false empowerment. Women of other races certainly feel protection from their men...those women are not the "back bones" of their communities.

I saw a billboard in a black community the other day and it pictured a BW with her two kids—I think it was advertising medical insurance. Then yesterday at the bookstore, I saw a book called "Black Mothers," depicting a mother on the cover with her young son and daughter. Backbone has gotten us single, below poverty, stressed, overweight, and depressed.

It seems that our community has reinforced the behavior assigned to that word. Where are our men in any of this. Should they not be the backbone? Hypothetically, in case of war, the backbone is what will hold you up. Are Black women to fight the men who are behind the wars? This has stripped some of our women of their femininity, dignity, and hope that we could depend on a man to be a man.

Mon Jan 29, 07:21:00 PM EST
Evia said...

> That statement made me think of one of your previous blogs about Mammies, Sapphires, and Jezebels. After reading that particular entry I began to see a lot of "mammy" in me (and coincidently in my mother as well—that's probably where I learned it).

Zabeth, that 'Mammy' role is a biggie! We could talk about that one role forever. Most black women play that role without a hitch. We play it so perfectly until we think it's just the way we are supposed to function. I see it in young black girls. I see it in adolescent girls and black females all the way to the nursing homes.

> I realized that I was giving way to much of myself and getting very little back in return. So now, I've become more focused on putting my needs and my happiness first.

You've got to be determined to do this because the whole community will be after you to stop being so 'selfish.' LOL! You've got to get ready for that, so that when they start, you'll have a plan and know exactly what you're going to say and do.

> BTW, this is kind of off topic but still very related. It has been simmering in the tabloid media that P-Diddy has been spotted spending a lot of cozy time with actress Sienna Miller, while Kim Porter, his current girlfriend (not wife)and mother of 3 of his five children (who by the way has just given birth to a set of twin girls) sits back at home. I know that that is kind of off topic but this really burns me. Why are so many BW willing to settle for this kind of treatment? If we truly are the backbone of the community than why don't we value ourselves enough to demand better?

Because a big part of the value of an AA woman to the black community comes from being a good 'Mammy.' A lot of the identity of many AA women is therefore interwoven into that role. Being a good Mammy is being that strong black woman with the backbone who keeps on keepin' on even when everybody abandons the ship. A good Mammy never cries out for help. She just sucks up her pain, loneliness, smiles, covers all of her bases and her man's too—if she has one—and her kids, her girlfriend's kids, her extended family, the community, the church, and on and on.

Some sistas I know have taken on 2nd and 3rd jobs to do this. And they still don't get appreciated because black folks believe that this is what a 'mammy' is supposed to do. They believe this is *normal* for African American women. Just think about what happens when an AA woman says, "I can't do anymore. I need help!" Well, everybody starts criticizing her and will call her a 'wimpy like a white woman' and she still won't get any help, sympathy, or support. LOL!

I had a mild problem with this myself. I didn't ask for help. I'd usually just try to bear whatever I'm going through all alone. My first husband used to get angry with me for that and Darren does too. They've said that makes them feel like I don't need them. So I've worked on that. I think real men primarily need to be needed, whereas women primarily want to loved."

Mon Jan 29, 09:06:00 PM EST

Zabeth said...

You've got to be determined to do this because the whole community will be after you to stop being so 'selfish.' LOL!

Oh, yes I've already started to experience that. LOL! Some of my friends are actually helping me and encouraging me to step out of my "I don't need any help" comfort zone and I am grateful to them for that.

Anywhoo, thank you so much for the advice in this area. And I do believe you are right, men do want to feel needed and women really just want to be loved.

10

Prison Inmate Lovers

August 10, 2006, 9:00 a.m.

As quiet as it is kept, some accomplished African American women are going into prisons to find a mate. They figure that if prison is where a disproportionate number of black men are, then this is where they need to go to find a man. I've personally known two well-educated, professional AA women to develop a *relationship* with a black man in prison. Actually, I worked with one of these women and heard frequent tidbits about this *romance*.

She got involved with him through her church that had a missionary program that went into prisons to visit inmates. She was wildly excited by his letters, which she said illustrated how intelligent he was. She even shared some of his letters with me. He had killed someone when he was eighteen and got a life term for the crime, however, there was a possibility that he would be released IF someone would help him with *this and that*.

I diplomatically advised her against this relationship. I had to choose my words carefully because when a woman is fishing for a man and hasn't had a nibble in years, and you can't tell her where else to find one, you're treading in shark-infested waters when you tell her to give up the man she's got on the hook—just because he's in prison for murder. So I listened to the excitement in her voice as she read his beautifully written letters. Oh, he also wrote short stories and stimulating poetry—some of the poems were quite titillating.

Sure this 36-year-old man sounded intelligent. He had gotten his GED and studied for a college degree while in prison. Of course, he hadn't gotten good legal representation during his trial, and definitely after 18 years in prison, he had a new outlook on life, but there was still a bad feeling in the pit of my stomach about this relationship.

Soon she began to send him money. He told her that he had been abandoned long ago by his family and friends and needed money for small expenses like cigarettes, candy, paper, clothes, etc. I didn't have a problem with her donating small amounts to his charity, but I did wonder how many other women were also receiving his poems and his letters requesting these donations.

Like a good gal pal, I listened to all the tidbits about the romance and the relationship woes. I held her hand and consoled her when he got upset with her because he felt she wasn't writing him often enough and wasn't trying hard enough to drum up enough support to get him another trial which he somehow hoped to do through getting a book of his short stories published.

Anyway, pretty soon, she was sharing her entire life with her "lover" telling him about all of her activities and about the people in her life, including me. She wanted me to talk with him in order to prove that she had found others who knew and cared about his plight. Now, it's only natural that a woman wants to share her family and friends with her man, but that's where I drew the line and told her that she shouldn't tell this man anything else about my family and me. I didn't want to hurt her, but she understood from the stern tone of my voice that I considered their relationship off the charts and that I didn't want to be involved in any *'ménage a trois.'*

She never mentioned him again. That was several years ago.

I was talking with her on the phone last night after a break in our relationship. She still doesn't have a man in her life and she hasn't dated anyone in the 12 years I've known her.

I don't know how widespread this phenomenon is of meeting men in prison, but this goes on (with all groups of women) and in some cases, AA women are marrying these inmates. The story of the second professional bw is similar. I also hear about some of these cases through other channels.

I'm speechless about this avenue that some black women are exploring for mates. Volumes have been written about women of all groups who mine the prisons for men. We've all heard of the women who fall in love with and marry infamous serial killers and other sociopaths/psychopaths. It's pretty bizarre to me, considering that there are so many quality men in the world. I know 'they' say you should "never say never," but, even if I never, ever found a man, I personally could never go that route. That, to me, is a recipe for disaster. I'd rather try to rob a bank and get shot to death. At least, I'd be out of my misery.

But this is one of the reasons I write this blog and urge black women to broaden their options to include ***all*** men of quality in the global village as dating and marriage options. It's easy for those around these women to tell them to keep praying for 'Mr. Right,' but without presenting these women with viable options, many AA women—who have been indoctrinated for centuries to mate only with AA men—are going to continue to look in the usual places and will continue to make poor relationship choices.

Posted by Evia at 8/10/2006 09:06:00 AM

COMMENTS:
Chr said...

Evia, yet again you have come up with a great topic. I was just watching something like this on TV. I am sorry but I have never considered any man with a criminal record as relationship material. The reasoning behind this is: 1) he is a criminal, 2) there is a chance he was exposed to HIV while in prison, 3) I deserve better. Like my grandmother and aunties used to say "I can do bad all by myself."

Thu Aug 10, 10:07:00 AM EDT
Evia said...

> *I am sorry but I have never considered any man with a criminal record as relationship material. . .*

Yeah, Chr, these women do deserve better! However, when folks are desperate, they'll resort to practically anything. As I pointed out, there've been stories about ww who 'fall in love' with and marry imprisoned killers and assorted inmates too. The difference is that some bw see bm inmates as a large "supply" of men just waiting to be tapped, and they believe that these men will appreciate them, love them, and be loyal, whereas you and I know that many of these guys are simply "users." More accomplished black women, like the women I referred to in my essay, tend to see these black male inmates as political prisoners, victims of an unjust racial, political system.

I haven't heard of anyone in the black community criticizing these women for doing this. Yet, look at the way many in the black community criticize black women who go the interracial route.

And for certain, contracting STDs is a *major* risk in getting sexual with an inmate, or a former inmate, for that matter. I don't know the exact circumstances, but some of the prisons do allow "conjugal "visits. I know a woman who's a social worker, and she said that some of her female clients actually go into the prisons for conjugal visits with their husbands.

Thu Aug 10, 11:22:00 AM EDT

Chr said...

Well like a male friend of mine says. "*Desperation smells worse than perspiration.*" These men can see it coming a mile away. Criminals normally are natural manipulators. So they are simply taking advantage of the situation. I get tired of people being critical of my relationship simply because my husband is white and I am black. No one has ever said anything but if looks could kill. . .

Thu Aug 10, 11:42:00 AM EDT

Ruminations of a Racial Realist (Clare) said..

> As quiet as it is kept, some accomplished African American women are going into prisons to find a mate.

While this is obviously a serious issue, one has to see the funny side! Your posts are sensational. You'll have to turn this blog into a book. I definitely think there will be a market for it in terms of the underlying theme of the blog i.e. black women needs to broaden their horizons to include non-black men.

My personal feeling is that although the situation is difficult for black women, that doesn't mean individual black women can't find "good black men." One has to remember that ok, even if 50% of African American doctors marry white women, that means that 50% are choosing black women (even though they could have a white woman if they wanted to) i.e. see the glass as half full instead of half empty. But your point of view makes for a really good debate on this issue, so yeah you should turn it into a book when you have enough posts!

Thu Aug 10, 11:58:00 AM EDT
Evia said...

Thanks Clare, for the kudos!

Sometimes, you do have to laugh to keep from bawling about this situation.

What's happening with your blog? Obviously our blogs approach this issue from different directions, but we're actually talking about the same thing, except I guess that I'm more of a 'black womanist' and focus on black women finding love and fulfillment and maybe the thrust of your blog is 'black love' in general.

> *My personal feeling is that although the situation is difficult for black women, that doesn't mean individual black women can't find "good black men." One has to remember that ok, even if 50% of African American doctors marry white women, that means that 50% are choosing black women (even though they could have a white woman if they wanted to) i.e. see the glass as half full instead of half empty.*

I agree that IF there are 50% of black men who prefer and choose black women, the glass is half-full, but I would rather not be one of the ones competing for those men. Maybe I just see things differently. I want a man to compete for me because I'm then in a better position to choose a better mate and father for my children.

Also, to me, it's unnatural. It goes against nature for black women to compete for males because the overwhelming majority of males in the animal kingdom compete for female attention—not the other way around. This is also the natural way of things among all cultures and societies of humans, except for maybe small, remote groups who are the subject of anthropological studies. So, I don't think AA women should even begin to try to work against nature.

Thu Aug 10, 01:39:00 PM EDT
Mimi said...

LOL, this topic is comical. I have personally heard this argument: 'black women with superior resources must reach back and save black men from the mire.' This also goes back to the coddling of black men. These dudes will be the first to tell you how the (white) man has them down, neglecting to mention the rape, robbery, murder, that they committed (often against another black person). These men sometimes have multiple women visiting them on different days. Given the rates of recidivism, I don't know why anyone would be interested.

This also suits the general pattern of many black women being in emotionally and physically distant relationship with black men. He is there in spirit but not in body. He asserts his will but is not there to support the family financially, emotionally, or any other ways the head of the house generally operates.

@Chr –

I agree these men know what to say to get what they want. It's sad that so many obviously intelligent women are that desperate for love and attention that they will look at a prisoner for marriage or companionship.

@Racialrealist –

50% of black doctors (and other professional black men) marry white women, and some other portions marry Asian, Hispanic, Indian, so the pot for black females is *less* than 50% and many of these men have (light) skin and (long/wavy/straight/anything but nappy) hair requirements when choosing a black woman.

Does anybody think religion plays a part? I have noticed a certain attitude more among Christians than any other group in the black community. Many black churches led by black men endorse suffering for black women and stress rewards that will be paid out in the distant future. They praise bw for 'going with the flow.' Don't cause waves, 'just pray and God will change it.' Muslims however tend to have a different attitude. They will pray but they will also take actions to accomplish their goal.

Thu Aug 10, 01:43:00 PM EDT
The Thinking Black Man said...
Hello Evia,

It really shouldn't be so bad for sistas that they have to resort to the brothers on lock-down. The very nature of prison generates a certain opportunity for scheme and scandal and most women will be well advised to pass on our incarcerated brothers, at least when it comes to trying to have a "relationship" while they are behind bars!

A member of my family got caught up in the "Black man is being oppressed by the white prison system..." hype. She befriended this guy and he escaped from prison, only to be caught 2 days later at his Mama's house. Then he was released like 18 months later. He wasn't supposed to leave the state but laws meant nothing to him. She sent him airfare, he went across country and acted like a damn fool in her place, and she had to ship him back to Mama. My point is that prison is a rough place, and men need time to get themselves together before they will be any good to a woman.

Adding to the interracial component of dating... as I was leaving work yesterday, I saw this couple on a bench. A white guy had his head in the lap of this amazing looking black woman and she was smiling at him and stroking his hair. I couldn't help but think, "I sure hope he appreciates her!" On the train home, I found myself wondering what put the two of them together: Brothers not stepping up to the plate? A poor impression of Brothers? Fate? Or a White Guy that had his s—t together? Regardless, I hope they were happy. I was going home to my amazing looking wife, so was he.

Thu Aug 10, 01:47:00 PM EDT
Evia said...

> *Well like a male friend of mine says, 'Desperation smells worse than perspiration.' These men can see it coming a mile away. Criminals normally are natural manipulators. So they are simply taking advantage of the situation. I get tired of people being critical of my relationship simply because he is white and I am*

black. No one has ever said anything but if looks could kill.

LOL @ 'Desperation smells worse than perspiration.'

Chile, just think about that—some of our own folk are mad at us for being in good relationships. (smh) Also, other black women should be real happy for sistas like you and me because we weren't in the so-called 'competition' for that small pool of quality AA men. I think many of us could pull one of those quality bm from that small pool because many bm say that *some* of the bw in interracial relationships tend to be the same type of women that many quality bm want. This is what many of the bm say who complain that wm are taking the *best* bw.

However, as I've often pointed out, I didn't marry a quality wm because I couldn't get a quality bm. At the time that I wanted to re-marry, Darren—a loving, loveable, suitable, and compatible man simply came along *first* and asked to marry me. I didn't see the point in refusing to be with a quality man like him in order to hold out for a quality bm, who may have come along the next day, a year later, ten years later, or possibly never. The only sure thing about this is that I would *only* have been interested in a quality bm. Quality and compatibility are, or ought to be, the key criteria for any woman in selecting a mate.

Less competition for quality black men makes it easier for bw who *only* want a bm, so those bw should be thrilled that we opted out of the 'competition.' Naturally, some bm aren't going to be happy about us leaving the fold, but they'll get over it. LOL!

My husband tries to make sure that he's there for me in the ways a loving mate is supposed to be, which is something that some of those folks who are giving us the evil eye can't digest. So, if the price for that is an evil look from time to time, that's real easy for me to handle!

The Thinking Black Man said...

@ Mimi-

CRISIS Magazine had a great article on Black Christian women suffering in the name of The Lord early this year or late last year!

The article was excellent, and sadly I know several women that basically fall under its purview. It is sometimes easy for brothers in the pulpit to stress to their Black female members, "Don't worry, Sister Sally, the Lord will give you a bountiful harvest on the oooother side of Glooory!" And often times, Sister Sally will just wait for it. I'm a Christian, folks, but damn that whole waiting thing!!! Sisters, I say "get yours **now** while you know what to do with it!!!"

I have heard some women in this position say, *"The Lord is MY Man"* and when I can, I tell them, "No, he's not! He's the Lord! He ain't bringing you roses, or baking salmon for you! He is not taking your car to the shop to get new brakes, and he is not rubbing your feet at the end of the day! Don't sit at home alone with your Bible waiting for Jesus to throw 'Mr. Right' through your front window! Damn all that sufferin' that Minister Jacobs was talking about! You better get up, get out, and see what the men are up to! It might be fun."

Thu Aug 10, 01:58:00 PM EDT
Evia said...

Mimi, as usual, your piercing eye didn't miss:

> *50% marry white, and some other portions marry Asian, Hispanic, Indian so the pot for black females is less than 50% and many of these men have (light) skin and long/wavy/straight/anything but nappy hair requirements when choosing a black woman.*

However, some of these same men will sex as many of these darker women as they can. Why? I heard one bm actually say on TV that he "practices" his sex techniques on the desperate women and that the fat girls (white or black) will allow a man to "do" them anyway he wants—so when he feels like going in the 'backdoor,' he looks for a fat girl.

Thu Aug 10, 02:14:00 PM EDT
Chr said...

I am a Christian too but the God I serve does not mean for me to be a fool. I know my husband is the man God meant for me because things have improved 10-fold for us after we got married. "He who finds a wife finds a good thing and obtains favor from the Lord." We have been together for 6 years and not once did I ever bring up marriage or beg him for a ring.

Thu Aug 10, 02:19:00 PM EDT
Evia said...

It really shouldn't be so bad for Sistas that they have to resort to the brothers on lock down.

Hey TBM, I agree, but many bw have been *indoctrinated* to be loyal to black men, feel really beaten down, and allow degrading things to happen to them and do degrading things out of desperation.

Mainly black folks in their family or the community—people who they *trust*—have constantly told them what's 'wrong' about them (complexion, hair, nose, lips, teeth, body size, attitude, etc.), until many of them feel unworthy and unlovable. This is another key factor. Virtually, any man who shows them attention has hit a home run under these circumstances because he tells them what's 'right' about them—at least until he can use them.

I hear what you say about these bw thumping their Bibles, but I'm happy they have that because don't you realize that the misery index would be a whole lot higher among AA women if it weren't for the black church, giving them a little bit of hope? A lot more of them would be doing degrading things; depression and health stats among them would be a lot worse; suicide rates would be higher, if it weren't for those ministers telling them to expect a pay-off in the by-and-by.

Thu Aug 10, 02:30:00 PM EDT
Mimi said...

Now, I am not disregarding Christianity in general. I am talking about the kind of Christianity that tends to get stressed in many black churches. God wants his servants to have a fulfilled life.

I sometimes went to my grandmother's church, and that place was a celebration. People looked joyful, the preacher would occasionally have a fire and brimstone sermon or some other serious topic, but man, when it was time to praise they were on it.

Going to other churches, the preachers stressed devotion, being long-suffering, and gratification in the afterlife. Everything is pray, and it will happen. Never pray *and* take steps. I mean basically, passiveness is preached to the women. There is no "God helps those who helps themselves attitude;" it's usually "Pray and if God grants it, you get it; if not, too bad." I think that is why at many churches there are so few men. Inaction and passiveness are not something many men would go for.

The same preacher was however fulfilling his wants and needs whether monetarily or sexually through the congregation. I can't tell you the amount of sexual sin and blatant fornication that occurs between some of the female members and male staff in some of these churches.

In regards to "practicing sex with black women," I have personally heard that so many times, it's ridiculous. 'I would never date you but I would sleep with you.' That attitude is why many black people below a certain age find it hard to believe that a man especially a non-black man can appreciate a black female as a total package beyond her sex and body shape. It's because bm constantly talk sex, sex, and more sex.

@tbm,

"the Lord is My man" is another attitude I dislike. It displays a lack of understanding about the fundamentals of Christianity and is such a crappy cover for the real problem.

@ Evia,

Don't even get me started. It amazes me that no black woman, no matter how beautiful or worthy is ever good enough for some of these men, yet they will get the ugliest, fattest, most slovenly non-black chick, flaunt her, and proclaim her from the highest mountain. I have had many non-black women who have a black man show a smug attitude around me or other black girls because of crap her man told her that trashes bw.

When my uncle introduced his 2nd wife, who was white, to our family, one of my more outspoken relatives asked if he divorced his beautiful black wife for that vagrant looking cow. His new wife is everything he claimed as a reason to divorce his first wife: vindictive, fat, lazy, bossy, demanding; yet he chose to marry this woman.

It's strange because out of other IR couplings, the only other combo where I noticed this disparity in looks is Asian female-white male pairs. Most other IRs are more matched.

Thu Aug 10, 03:49:00 PM EDT

Anonymous said...

To clarify, some of these women replace their unhealthy relationship with mortal men by having an unhealthy and non-Bible based relationship with God or preachers—or co-dependency.

Here's a book: *"Holy Lockdown: Does the Church Limit Black Progress?"* by Jeremiah Camara and an excerpt from it:

> *[Stone Mountain, GA (BlackNews.com) - More than half of all black people in the United States attend church on a regular basis and nearly 82% are members of churches. Currently, there are approximately 85,000 predominantly black churches in the United States. Blacks could have 1,700 churches in every state. The Black church is a 50 billion-dollar asset business and rakes in over 3 billion dollars annually. Why is it that blacks are amongst the most Jesus-praising people on earth, yet the most fragmented and economically dependent? Is there a correlation between high praising and low productivity? Why are there many churches yet major problems in black communities? The church is the leader of the black community by default.]*

Camara contends that many Black preachers are routinely delivering sermons that keep the black collective in a state of powerlessness and that "Holy Lockdown" is an interpretation of what many Blacks are feeling toward the church but don't quite know how to express their frustrations."Holy Lockdown" takes a critical look at the collective impact the church has made on the black psyche, and it explores the possibility of the church as being a contributing factor to the many social problems facing blacks.

Here is another excerpt from the book:

> *["Expressive displays of emotion are good and can be therapeutic, but must lead to a practical place over time. We have to have religion with reason and emotion with a purpose."]*

About the Author: Jeremiah Camara has studied the idioms, language, and culture of predominately black churches of various denominations for over a decade. His diligent research and insightful perceptions are thoroughly presented throughout this timely and much anticipated work.

"*Holy Lockdown: Does the Church Limit Black Progress?*" is catching fire in many parts of the country. It is a topic worthy of discussion.

For more information, please visit www.twelvehp.com
PRESS CONTACT:
Jeremiah Camara
888-504-0999
camara12@bellsouth.net
Thu Aug 10, 04:06:00 PM EDT

Heavenly Zeta said...

Wow...good topic, Evia! It's something that hit home for me. One of my very dear friends is currently engaged to a man that spent (I think) 8 years or so in prison for a felony drug conviction. Of course, he has a hard time finding gainful employment, etc., lives with her, etc. (and she's known him less than a year). This same friend was previously involved with a guy who was *finishing* a prison term for—yep, a felony drug conviction. That, of course, went south as soon as he got out. I mean, he returned to his old ways within 2 weeks of his release.

Now, she's one of those headstrong, "I'mma do what I want to do" folks, so it does me no good to tell her she could do so much better. She was also desperate for a relationship, so like most black women, she took the first thing that showed her some interest, despite the fact that he doesn't have much to offer. Sad state, I tell ya, sad state...

Thu Aug 10, 05:00:00 PM EDT

Shavonne said...

Sc$%w that! I'll be damned if I date someone that's locked up. That's desperation at its worst. My philosophy is: Once you go to prison/jail, the relationship is so over!

11

Sabotage Again—Do Black Women Push White Men Away?

May 22, 2007

Picture: #1—Prince Maximilian of Liechtenstein and Princess Angela

Picture: #2—Prince Max and Princess Angela of Liechtenstein

Picture: #3—Prince and Princess of Liechtenstein and son, Alfons
Princess Angela (Formerly Angela Brown) and Prince Maximilian of Liechtenstein were married on January 29, 2000. Prince Maximilian is reported to have a trust fund worth 1 billion dollars. This couple has one son, Alfons.)

Picture: #4—Count Ferdinand Von Hapsburg and Countess Mary

The African woman in picture #4 is Sudanese and is now married to Count Ferdinand von Hapsburg, European Royalty. Her name is Mary Nuanut Macher. They have 3 children who also bear the title of Count/Countess. In America, most of us know that many black men would shun this woman due to her dark chocolate skin shade. Yet a blue blood royal found her beautiful, desirable, married her, and elevated her to the role of Countess of Austria.

These black women did *not* push these loving and loveable, suitable and compatible white men away!

Black women, a few months ago, we addressed the issue of why many white men may hesitate to ask a black woman out or why a lot more white men never approach black women, or compliment us. Many of you have declared that this is proof positive that most white men don't find black women attractive, or are not interested in dating black women. I've always countered that this is not true. Many white men are very interested, but a big factor in their seeming lack of interest these days is the less-than receptive attitude of many black women.

I decided to revisit this issue after receiving the comments below in yesterday's comments from a white man about the issue of why more white men don't show more interest in black women. What he's saying here is important. His comments speak to the very heart of this issue. I think or rather I *know* that what he says here is a major reason why some white men don't show open interest in black women these days, or the same as they would other women.

Anyway, he says:

> *As a white man I would feel comfortable dating a black woman, except there is something that I hear way too much and seems to be behind a lot of black woman-white male relationships. I get the feeling that if there was not a black man shortage or other problems with black men, most black females would not give a white or non-black men the time of day. I hear comments like 'I've only dated dark-skinned black men and "black men aren't into dark skin black females so... I'll give a non-black man a chance. No white guy, or any other man, wants to feel like a consolation prize because no black man was available. Would you feel at least a little bit of trepidation if so many white men told you "I've only white women, but since they're not giving me the time of day. . . ..*

I'm so happy for his comments because in general I don't think that most bw realize the way some of the public statements made about this issue affect wm who may indeed be very interested in dating bw. I've pointed out that when a typical wm hears and reads constantly on the internet, TV, radio, magazines, etc. from bw versions of: "I love my black man or my black king," or "Nothing but a black man!" or "There is no man like a black man," and the rude and crude "I don't want no white boy!" and on and on, this turns many white men away from even thinking about approaching a black woman.

Add to that the constant wailing that *some* bw do about bm with ww or other non-bw, then I can easily see how *any* white man, Hispanic man, Asian man, etc. would not think that such women are interested in any other man but a black man unless she's a desperado. Naturally, no man wants to be latched onto out of desperation or 2nd choice! Yet many of these same women will say to me and others in a matter of fact way: "wm don't approach us bw" or "wm don't find us attractive," or "wm don't want bw except for sex." LOL!

I realize that many black women are going through a transition phase regarding this issue as they shift their focus from a single group of men to *all* of the men in the global village. Unfortunately, our talk with each other about this transition is getting a worldwide broadcast on the internet. In this respect, I've often wondered how some of what I and others say here may be interpreted because I know that many white and other men are reading this and raising their eyebrows. The thing is that most bw don't have anywhere else to talk about this virtually taboo (in some quarters) transition. I'm sure that groups of other women can talk about this topic in their friendship circles or other places in their community, but most black women don't have the courage or the support among other black women to do this in their locale.

In a day and time in which Asian women are openly rejecting Asian men and explicitly stating that they want to marry a white man and many white and some Hispanic women are going out of their way to catch a black man's eye—even if some of these women only want a "chocolate experience,"—it's apparent to me that black women are not availing themselves of many dating experiences with good men out there of other skin shades.

I've begun to notice the openly flirtatious behavior of young, non-black women towards bm. For ex., I was at the craft store yesterday and these two young white female cashiers became extremely animated when a youngish black male approached the checkout counter. They became hyper-bubbly, started showing him a lot of teeth even before he got to the counter and their shoulders and other body parts began to wiggle. (I knew exactly what these moves meant because I'm a woman.) They were flirtatious with him throughout the whole transaction, as he paid for his items. There aren't that many black males in that area, so I guess he was a novelty to them. Anyway, he was cool about it all, but I could tell that he was keenly aware of their interest, and I'll bet he'll be going back into that store—and real soon! Anyway, I wondered how differently and in what ways this would have played if the women had been black and the guy, white.

So, in addition to often-shrill proclamations rejecting white and other non-bm, many AA women don't show even subtle interest in white and other men which reinforces in the mind of the non-bm that black women are *not* interested in them. Many AA women are turning off hordes of potentially interested non-black men in these ways. All heterosexual men are most interested in friendly, "win-able" women or women who they perceive they are able to "win" or get. As some black women here have said, the message from the shrill group can be embarrassing and amounts to pure *sabotage* for those bw who are very interested in broadening their options.

Additionally, my 30-year-old black male relative pointed out another scheming reason why so many black men continue to discourage black women from dating other men. He said those black men *know* that many black women are desirable to white and other men because men know what other men want. However, the reason why many bm continue to vehemently oppose black women dating non-bm is for an often overlooked reason.

He said they know that if bw start dating out in droves, that in itself will *devalue* black men at a time when—lo and behold, black men are becoming more desirable to other groups of women. He said that even though the number of single bw can be 80%, 90%, even 100%, most black men are going to continue to plant distrust in bw's minds about wm and other non-black men in order to turn bw away from the interracial option. He said black men want their value to continue to rise and they want to maintain it, and it can only continue rising and stay high if black females continue to want a *black man only*. To use an economic model, high interest = high value.

High demand for any commodity pushes up the value, so this is a simple case of 'supply and demand.' After all, if it gets out that your women are leaving you, you can't be that desirable, just as many Asian men are depicted.

So, BINGO! In addition to enjoying the attention of a surplus of 'black man only' black women pursuing them, this is also why a lot of so-called "good" black men are quiet about some of the verbal attacks in cyberspace and the media that denigrate black women. As the value of black women goes down in the public eye, many bw are unable to use their lowered value as leverage to bargain for higher quality mates, which makes these women easier for *any* bm (even the so-called "good" bm) to get or keep around for no-strings sex or a bm's fall-back woman aka *safety net*. As one bw said, "Even homeless bm these days think they can get a bw who's an executive."

The bottom line is that many of the bm in the so-called "decent" or "good black man" category are *also* privately enjoying the current high demand for bm, in more ways than one. Could this be a key reason why they're so quiet about the rampant use and abuse of bw by damaged beyond repair black men? Hmmmm . . . .

Black women, you've simply got to move on and stop looking back.

Posted by Evia at 5/22/2007 06:37:00 AM

12

Alec Wek, Black Female Beauty and White Men

January 21, 2007, 9:15 a.m.

Here are some pictures of supermodel, Alec Wek.

- **Pictures : Alec Wek**

Of course, Alec Wek's SO (significant other/husband) is a white man! Duh!

A very large proportion of black men, throughout the Western world, would absolutely *not* be attracted to a woman with Alec Wek's complexion, hair texture, and facial features. Of course, I've heard about and witnessed a lot of this black male dislike or aversion to dark skinned, non-euro-looking or less euro-looking black females all of my life. I've heard numerous AA males either say about Alec that she's ugly, unattractive, or they'll be very silent—either ashamed or scared to talk—when they're asked how they think she looks. LOL!

However, if everything about Alec were kept the same except she were white, many of these same black men would be very interested. Let's say if she had the same broad cheekbones, small eyes, beautiful smile, but with peach-colored skin and long platinum blond or any color of Euro hair, do you believe many bm would reject her?

Some white men, on the other hand, are able to see Alec's beauty—often called "exotic"—just as she is, just like they see the beauty in many white, black, and other women who don't fit the very narrow definition of Madison Avenue's view of female beauty. Why is it that so *many* black men cannot appreciate Alec's so-called "exotic" beauty? It's because many black men have an *aversion* to the looks of less-euro looking black women.

Beauty is not a fact; it's an opinion. Yes, we've all heard that "beauty is in the eye of the beholder," or an *opinion*, but many people still regard it as a fact. For ex. many people think it's a fact that Halle Berry is beautiful, but that's simply an opinion held by many people who've been infused with an indoctrination program.

At any rate, to get back to the specific topic of this blog, I've said this several times before: A large number of white men (these days) and *some* other non-black men have opinions about female beauty that differ from the Madison Avenue standard. Great! This means that there are many white men and some other non-black men who are definitely looking at the beauty of "typical African American women" and are able to appreciate a *much* wider range of black female beauty than the majority of black men I've encountered, heard about, or read about.

Note that I didn't say that there aren't some AA men who adore dark-skinned black women, but wouldn't you *expect* a very high percentage of upwardly mobile, well-positioned AA men to "prefer" the beauty of darker black women or more typical African American women? Instead, they don't and this is clearly seen by the women who upwardly mobile, better-positioned AA men pursue, date, cohabit with, or marry. Their behavior is the opposite of the behavior of virtually every other group of men in the world, in this regard. Therefore, it is abnormal behavior.

Typical, well-positioned men of other groups overwhelmingly pursue, date, and marry the women in their group. They *exalt* the looks of the bulk of their women—and not the minority of women who look the least like the bulk. Unlike the majority of AA males, the vast bulk of men in the world do not discriminate against the women in their group who look the most like their ancestors.

Naturally, many AA males go into denial and will argue that their preference for lighter black women like Beyonce and Megan Good does not matter because these women are "black" too. Some of them can become vehement about this and argue for days trying to justify their discriminatory behavior because they know their behavior is not normal and is actually racist. They do not want their abnormal behavior pattern revealed.

However, when any black man shuns or refuses to date or marry a black woman with a darker skin shade on the basis of her skin shade and/or other stereotypic African features, like a wider nose, or tighter-coiled hair, this is gendered racism. At its most basic level, racism = depriving people of privileges based on skin shade (primarily) and/or descent. These darker black women are being denied the privilege of being asked out and ultimately this affects the chances of marriage for these women. After all, a man typically dates a woman before he marries her. Fewer dates = less likelihood of marriage for the woman. Fewer dates = fewer choices to select a *quality* man.

When black men with greater resources like higher education, influence, money, power, etc. reject the more stereotypic African looking woman, the effect of the discrimination is compounded because not only are those women denied fewer options for marriage, they are also denied access to the privileges that these resources provide.

Yes, all men reject some of the women in their group and for a variety of reasons. However, the discrimination I refer to here, only comes into play when bm base their rejection of black women on dark skin and stereotypic African features like nose shape and hair texture. This is *intra-racism, but it's still racism.*

Many black men heap venom on me for pointing out their hypocrisy concerning this issue of discriminating against darker, more stereotypic African looking black women because they love to castigate whites for discriminating against them and want no comparison to what they also do towards darker black women. But how is the discrimination that a large percentage of black men perpetrate against darker women any different? Please ask them that.

Of all the issues I write about, I've gotten the most mail from virulently angry black men about this issue of black male "colorism" or gendered racism. They know it's vile and don't want it talked about because they still want dark women to support them in various ways, or as comrades.

Of course, they claim it's just a matter of "preference" for lighter-whiter women. Well, racist white people *also* have a "preference" for lighter people too—other white people.

The wider range of beauty appreciated by *some* white men is proven by the choice of black women (photos on my site) they choose as significant others and for the purpose of this blog, the ones they choose to love and marry.

I know this may be a surprise to some people, but many black people were mentally poisoned to death by forced miscegenation that occurred during slavery and in particular, miscegenation's offspring: colorism. These black people absolutely cannot see *any* beauty in a black woman who looks like Alec Wek, mainly because of her complexion, features, and her hair. However, some of these black people do not believe they've been poisoned. They fully believe that the way they think about black beauty is "normal." SMH

For sure, many black males of various ages will proclaim loudly, as I've heard them, that Alec is "ugly," or Whoopi Goldberg is "not attractive," etc. So I deliberately used the word "poisoned" because millions of black people are killing each others' spirit because of colorism.

Has anyone else noticed how so many black folks (a la D.L. Hughley and Damon Wayans) are always on the lookout for "ugly" black women and most of these so-called "ugly" black women have one thing in common: dark complexions. Or in some cases, "ugly" to these males = a dark complexion and a stereotypic West African nose shape and tightly coiled hair, also known as "nappy." This stuff is too sad for words. Lawdy!

Now ponder this: Many black men, particularly those in the U.S. and to a lesser extent, some black women, make the most important decision that a person can make, namely, the choice of a mate with whom they will reproduce, based on skin shade *alone*. Others look also at whether the person's hair has a tight curl (nappy), loose curl, or is straight. And of course, many other less-important decisions are based on features such as these.

Now what has a person's complexion or tightness of hair curl got to do with the *quality* of that person? *Nothing.* But when you have millions of people (AAs and others) basing their most important decisions on those two traits, that's a recipe for backwardness and self-destruction.

Yes, many whites base many of their decisions on those two traits too, and this is known as racism when they deny privileges to blacks based on our skin shade and African ancestry. But whites, as a group, *gain* from doing that. African Americans *lose* enormously from doing it. Many African Americans still can't see that they lose when they discriminate against blacks the same as whites. So, do you see another major reason why AAs aren't making progress that other groups make? Here's a prediction: African Americans will never make any significant progress *as a group* as long as they engage in this kind of stupid, group-destructive, discriminatory behavior. Yet, many AAs want other groups to respect and embrace them. Please!

When I've talked to various white people about this type of intra-racial discrimination that blacks perpetrate against each other based on skin shade and hair, they're surprised. Many of them absolutely cannot grasp that, because they view *all* black people as black or as being non-white, just as AAs view *all* white people as white. It's hard for whites to focus on skin shade differences among us unless there is a striking difference because it's not important to them in *most* cases. This explains why many wm who date bw will find a chocolate-skinned black woman just as attractive as he would a caramel-skinned or lighter one. The fact is that if a wm prefers light-bright-white women with long, straight hair, he most likely won't be interested in AA women because typical AA women are browner or darker and don't have straight hair.

I remember the first time I heard some white co-workers talking about a "dark" white person with "olive" skin. That was a mystery to me, but I kept quiet and listened. It took me a while to figure out what they were talking about. I still have a problem differentiating the different skin shades of whites. The same goes for whites when differentiating average black skin shades.

Intra-racism or "colorism" is yet another serious barrier to progress for AAs (and certain other black groups too). It's a hidden, self-erected barrier, but it's a rock-solid one because it's active, and it's active everywhere. This is one of the reasons why many white people and others cannot understand what's holding black people back from progressing like other non-whites in the U.S., in terms of aggressively taking advantage of opportunities in this country. Most white people and even many other ethnic blacks do not understand the depth, insidiousness, and very wide-ranging impact, of colorism (and self-hate based on African ancestry) on the self-concept and therefore, the self-esteem of blacks in their day-to-day functioning.

At any rate, since such a large proportion of AA males continue to use such a bogus standard to determine female beauty and overlook high-quality black females everyday as they search for *only* those females with a lighter/whiter skin shade and so-called "soft" features, it's only a matter of time before the group is finished. This is because *quality* is what enables people to survive and thrive—not skin shade, nose shapes, and hair length or texture. I make it a point to distance myself and have always tried to distance my children from any black person (man or woman) who thinks this way because IMO, this is proof positive of self-hate and lack of pride in their heritage. It also indicates a lack of *survive-and-thrive intelligence.*

When confronted about their discriminatory actions, many African American men use the defense: "I can't help myself because the white man taught us to hate or devalue dark skin!" (SMH) Many of these men declare this in an arrogant fashion, as if to say that because someone told them a lie, they will keep repeating it even when it ends in their own destruction and that of the women and children of their group. Is there any word or term that can adequately capture how pathetically sad that is? If you can think of such a word, please send it to me because I plan to use it quite a bit. I'm serious.

Personally, I see the color or shade of a person's complexion the way I see their clothing. Their complexion is just like the color of the clothes they wear because skin only covers the outer portion of a person. Skin shade has *nothing* to do with the interior of a person or their quality or their beauty, or lack of it.

Seen this way, Alec Wek wears dark brown outfits (her skin) all of the time, accentuated by other colors (articles of clothing).

Just "think" about what that's like for dark brown women—having millions of black men discriminating against you simply because you wear dark brown outfits and keep in mind that many of these men wear dark brown all of the time themselves!

Black folks and others who harbor self-hate: You *can* change your thinking, if you want. The antidote that my white husband offers to black men whose minds have been poisoned against the wide range of black female beauty:

> *Re-train yourselves to see quality, beauty, and desirability in black women of all complexions, facial features, and hair textures. Period.*

Posted by Evia at 1/21/2007 09:37:00 AM

COMMENTS:
Meli said...

Your topic choices are always so powerful Evia! I don't know one black American person who is unaffected (good or bad) by this matter in our community. Your husband Darren has the right idea, but black men won't ascribe to it. Sadly, there is a reward for ascribing to the narrow views of beauty. Some of the males are learning this garbage at such a young age. I know that we all have a choice of whom we date/mate/marry, but why the negative stuff? It's essentially intra-racial prejudice. If Michael Jackson isn't reason enough for us to re-train our thinking, nothing is. MJ literally mutilated himself surgically, bleached his skin, and straightened and dyed his hair to the point of androgyny! All this because of shame! Yet we still perpetuate this! It is especially difficult for black women who fall outside the accepted hues of blackness. It is no wonder why so many black women refuse to venture outside the race for dating. If your own does not affirm you, then who will? Luckily, we are beginning to see daily proof that we are desired by other men.

Sun Jan 21, 06:00:00 PM EST

Meli said...

In case I wasn't clear, I want to add that by ascribing to narrow views of beauty, black men feel that they are dating or marrying up. They feel that they are getting better quality, so to speak, based on/depending on a black woman's skin shade. Although, sometimes skin shade goes out the window as long as she meets other Eurocentric beauty standards.

Sun Jan 21, 06:06:00 PM EST

Shavonne said...

I can't help myself because the white man taught us to hate or devalue dark skin.' (SMH) Is there any word or term that can adequately capture how pathetically sad that is?

Poppycock. I like to use the word when I hear or read something so totally ridiculous and sad.
Sun Jan 21, 07:29:00 PM EST

Evia said..

I don't know one black American person who is unaffected (good or bad) by this matter in our community.

Yes, this is true and this is one of the main reasons why the AA group's progress is so slow or actually regressing. Colorism and other self-hate issues are interwoven into the negative self-concept that many AAs have as individuals and as a group. The self-concept that a person has is at the core of their being. It underlies *everything*. It's all intertwined. It is the reason why many AAs don't take advantage of the opportunities here that some black immigrants come here and use to sail past us. It plays heavily in the infighting and divisions among AAs. Other black immigrants also have some self-hate issues, but when they come to the U.S., their issues tend to play out in less destructive ways.

The bottom line is that there just aren't *enough* AAs who have a positive self-concept or pride in themselves and our group to move the group forward at this point. Of course, many will say the white man taught us to hate ourselves. That is such a cop-out—as if they can't unlearn anything that they may have been taught IF they want to unlearn it. As you say, some AAs don't want to unlearn it. It's so much easier to shift the blame to *'de evil white man'* (white folks) and continue to complain, as if anyone cares. What has never made sense to me about all of the complaining is that since 'de evil white man' is so evil (according to this *logic*)—then surely 'de evil wm' doesn't care. So what is the point of continuing to yap about 'de evil white man?'

With all of the books, the internet, classes, discussion groups, etc., there is an abundance of information about all of the major contributions that blacks have made and are yet making to all areas of life. There are so many reasons to be filled with pride about being a so-called "black" American person. This is a big part of the re-training process that Darren talks about. Nobody is stopping anyone from reading anything they want. If more AAs read a lot more, we'd all be a lot better off. The fact is that many blacks in America don't want to change their thinking.

Sun Jan 21, 08:21:00 PM EST

Las said...

Hi Evia, I remember how I brought her up some months back. I felt bad putting her down, but I was being honest and it made me think about my own standards. I was stunned, yet a little relieved knowing that Alec is with a White male (too weird to explain). Thanks for sharing that.

> *I've heard about and witnessed a lot of this black male dislike or aversion to dark skinned, non-euro-looking or less euro-looking black females all of my life, and I've heard numerous AA males either say about Alec that she's ugly, unattractive, or they'll be very silent—either ashamed or scared to talk—when they're asked how they think she looks.*

I mentioned on another blog I think it's so interesting that some black men claim "one" of the reasons they date non-black is because black women "ask too much of them" or "don't want them" because of low or no income, lack of education, previous incarcerations, or children all over the place, etc. (I know these don't apply to all). But most of them initially reject most black women because they don't fit society's beauty standard—too dark, too over-weight etc. So it seems it's only acceptable for them to have choices and options when choosing women. And we're not allowed to have choices or standards for ourselves, if they approach us for companionship.

> *I know this may be a surprise to many people, but many black people have been mentally poisoned to death by that forced miscegenation (that occurred during slavery) and in particular, miscegenation's offspring: colorism.*

Just the other day I had a conversation with an older White female colleague about this issue. She brought up Tiger Woods and his wife having a baby soon (as if I would care). I began to tell her the "history" about colorism and self hate. She didn't think it applied to Tiger (go figure). So, for a better example I mentioned MJ's physical changes and the choices he made to have non-black surrogate mothers. She seemed shocked and still tried to tell me that he has a skin "disease" and those kids are biologically his, but he may have suppressive white genes that showed up. I got so frustrated, I stayed distant from her out of annoyance throughout the entire afternoon (and that's not like me to do). So much I want to say, but my contacts are killing me and I need to hit the sack.

Sun Jan 21, 10:41:00 PM EST

Meli said...

You are right, Evia. All we have to do is read, whether by Internet or getting a library card and hitting up the public libraries. We need to do that because with all the very negative images we see of ourselves, the awesome achievements made by those before us and currently will trump that unflattering stuff. Instead, we wait until February (Black History month) to host "programs" at the church to honor our trailblazers and essentially, our own spirits. We need this type of affirmation at least weekly.

I agree that some in our community have been most critical of Alec Wek since she came on the super modeling scene. I tell you Evia, if we had to rely solely on validation from black folks overall, we would be some depressed women. LOL! Meanwhile, awesome Alec is crying all the way to the bank. I am just troubled that there are not more models like her on the runway, period—*black* models period!

I have to say that what I admire about Tyra Banks is that she is honest about what it takes to get her 'look.' She admits to wearing a ton of weave, layers of make-up, and special undergarments (Spanx) to hide cellulite and thick thighs. She is real. She was brave enough to show herself/pics "unaltered" and then the air brushed versions. Aisha Tyler also did that in a magazine that she was featured in. She showed her natural self and then how the pictures were digitally altered to make her look perfect.

I think that all men are guilty of falling for the "dream," but they always wake up to reality. I know we cannot change BM, but we can ignore the hell out of them and stop supporting what does not support us.

Which is why I don't understand why BW damn near deify BM—especially the ones who cross over at alarming rates!

Sun Jan 21, 10:59:00 PM EST

Halima said...

I prefer Clara Benjamin myself:

-http://www.ferideuslu.com/pics/rf.clara_500_60.jpg

because I think Alec's cheeks can get too round.

-http://www.taketwo-model.com/models/girls/clara_benjamin/page_02.html

Also I think Alec isn't in modeling because of what is seen as conventional 'beauty' anyway so I can understand some reservation towards her, but I think she gets a hard time because people have placed the burden of 'representative of race' on her shoulder. Black people are afraid that she will contribute to the negative stereotypes and ideas of Africans, but strangely enough, this is because white people have historically used such features seen on Africans to depict stupidity etc, not because they are markers of such in themselves!

I am glad I find that I can appreciate beauty as found on the continent. I was on a bus once and a girl (looking just like Clara) and her mum got on. I tell you I stared like there was no tomorrow!

I understand where it comes from but it is very sad that black folk can't enjoy a thing without wondering how whites are viewing it!

Without this constant consciousness of what white folks would think, a lot of us would have better mental health.

http://dateawhiteguy.blogspot.com/

Mon Jan 22, 05:57:00 AM EST

Las said...

> *Also I think Alec isn't in modeling because of what is seen as conventional 'beauty' anyway so I can understand some reservation towards her, but I think she gets a hard time because people have placed the burden of 'representative of race' on her shoulder. Black people are afraid that she will contribute to the negative stereotypes and ideas of Africans, but strangely enough, this is because white people have historically used such features seen on*

> *Africans to depict stupidity, etc, not because they are markers of such in themselves!*

Halima, I feel this too. However, at first I felt she was initially put there to make a "mock" of African beauty or to somehow "uplift" the White models based on our already biased standards. Even so, all races of people have considered some of their own as "unattractive." So I felt she was just an unattractive woman who happens to be black. She doesn't even resemble the majority of African women in Africa. Yet, it's not fair she gets that burden of representation. But I can't help but to feel it was deliberately designed that way. This is where my resentment comes in, but I admire her for her strength. I could imagine the painful remarks she gets from people including her own.

Mon Jan 22, 08:10:00 AM EST

Evia said...

> *Also I think Alec isn't in modeling because of what is seen as conventional 'beauty' anyway so I can understand some reservation towards her,*

Halima, what really is *beauty*? Let's remember that in the current world, white people decide who's beautiful and who's not. As a result of the white supremacist overlay on the entire world, white people determine the standards. The case of Alec Wek's beauty is a prime example of that. I think that the boundaries of 'beauty' are being expanded in her case. After all, 'conventional white female beauty' has never been rigid. It has changed considerably throughout history among white people. For ex. look at the fat Rubenesque "beauties" in the paintings by Rubens. In those days, the 'Rosie O'Donnell' type of body would have been considered beautiful or very sexy.

What we know of female beauty in the Western world today is simply a "construct" made up of a bunch of the opinions of white men, mostly. So now, powerful white (alpha) men have decided that for whatever reason, they want to expand the boundaries to include the type of look that Alec Wek has. They've put their stamp of approval on her to the extent that I'll bet she had many white men pursuing her and other white men—at least European men—are pursuing other black women who have some of the same characteristics as her.

Ever since I started dating wm, I've been noticing the women that many—even rich and influential white men, date and marry. Have you ever noticed these women? These women, in many cases, are not beautiful—by the narrow Madison Avenue ideal of conventional white beauty standards. Yet many (not all) white men are apparently conditioned to think for themselves enough to see the beauty in these women, and they don't have to be concerned about whether anyone else on earth thinks their woman is beautiful because, after all, they set the standards that other men try to copy!

Many non-white men, on the other hand, are very concerned with whether others will think that their woman is beautiful enough, or thin enough, or "fine" enough, etc. because they constantly seek the approval of the status quo of their surroundings that is heavily influenced by what wm have decided. If white men decide that Alec Wek's beauty is within the confines of what's beautiful, it's a done deal, and it's only a matter of time before black men and other men will begin to see her and women who look similar to her as more attractive, more desirable.

Mon Jan 22, 09:02:00 AM EST

Anonymous said...

One of the reasons why this reality is not openly discussed in the black community, IMO, is because it in essence proves that what racist whites have been saying for centuries is correct. The real desire for equal rights—at least from a black male perspective—was to have equal access to white women without being lynched. Nothing more.

It was not about uplifting and helping the community as a whole to take advantage of hard-earned opportunities—a desire that most black women thought the Civil Rights movement was naturally about.

Black males have always been thought of by white racists (and the world at large) as immature, led by their emotions instead of intellect, irresponsible, easily influenced, etc. The list goes on. Just look at the skyrocketing out-of-wedlock birthrate, the often abandonment of full black children black males produce, the low level of educational accomplishment, high level of involvement in criminal activities, and the prison system. Just look at the misogyny directed at black women, and just imagine the astounding amount of *self-hate* that must be involved in the astronomically high numbers of young black males viciously killing each other.

Basically, they're trying to kill their own hated image. It all adds up to a large number of black males who are psychically, psychologically, and numerically lost.

Do *all* fit this description? Of course not. It would be a lie to claim any such thing. However those who are marriage and father material are by and large (there *are* exceptions of course) in the minority. They are also colorist and would not give the average black woman (unless she has physically detectable white, Asian, or Indian admixture) the time of day, no matter how much she has to offer—all because of her less-Euro color, features, and hair-texture.

This is a fact and is one of the reasons why IMO black Americans as a group will never excel and reach the same level of independence, financial, and familial health that other groups have in this society and world. Any community or culture containing males (I reserve the title "men" for protectors, providers, and supporters of their women) that have such disdain and disregard for its female members based on physical features that are typical of (and natural for) its population is doomed.

Thank you, Evia, for continuing to write about these taboo issues that need to be openly acknowledged and discussed.

The beautiful thing is that the growing numbers of black women worldwide, in the entertainment industry, business, and all walks of life are loving—and allowing themselves to be loved by—non-black men who don't have such narrow definitions of beauty. Yes, growing numbers of women of color are finally and unapologetically allowing their own needs to supersede the needs of the "community".

God bless us.

Mon Jan 22, 09:41:00 AM EST

Ms CPA said...

Almost none of the models on the runway these days have conventionally pretty faces, so I thought Alec was just another unconventional face on the scene. I am always happy to see another black woman with short nappy hair (I don't consider "nappy" to be a negative way to describe our hair). I certainly never thought that she was selected as a model to mock black or African beauty. Her husband is quite attractive, I would have been shocked beyond belief if he were black, knowing what I know about how black men view us.

Mon Jan 22, 10:07:00 AM EST

Evia said...

> One of the reasons why this reality is not openly discussed in the black community, IMO, is because it in essence proves that what racist whites have been saying for centuries is correct. The real desire for equal rights - at least from a black male perspective - was to have equal access to white women without being lynched. Nothing more. It was not about up-lifting and helping the community as a whole to take advantage of hard earned opportunities—a desire that most black women thought the Civil Rights movement was naturally about.

Anonymous! You've said a 'mouthful' here, as my grandmother used to say. This provokes a lot of thought! Whew! This statement is a whole blog or book, in itself.

It is certain that black men and black women are very different in this regard if you look at what they pursue. I've noticed this too, but I don't know why. When you consider that bm and bf grow up together in the same households, why are we *so* different? How could this happen? Anyway, these are rhetorical questions that I'm not sure whether any bw can answer. It would take some very honest bm to adequately address this issue.

I've noticed online that when bm do try to tell the truth, bw jump on them and begin judging them, which makes the men get quiet or go away.

I know that it hurts like hell, and I don't like to see black women hurting, but they're hurting like that anyway. I think the time has come for black women to get the emotional grit they need in order to hear the lowdown on how bm really feel. And after listening, the women should thank the men. The way I see it is that this is an opportunity for bw to be released—freed to go forth, explore, and find new horizons and new men in the global village who are able to uphold, protect, and value bw.

I agree with you that the average black woman thought that the Civil Rights movement and all the battles since were about equal access to opportunities (education, health, housing, employment, higher quality life for family, children, etc.) and equal protection before the law. I realize now I have no idea what black men thought it was all about. I just made an assumption it was the same for them.

But I always watch what people do when they have a choice, and when we look at the behavior of numerous AA and other black males these days who have the choice to select the woman they want from among all hues of women, more often than not, many of them are selecting white, white-skinned, or more euro-looking women. It's a pattern. Obviously, freedom and "overcoming" for these men meant having access to whiter women. Patterns are not accidental. One thing I know for sure is that black women definitely didn't think they were fighting to provide greater access to whiter or white women for black men.

Mon Jan 22, 10:14:00 AM EST
Evia said...

> *I don't consider "nappy" to be a negative way to describe our hair. I certainly never thought that she was selected as a model to mock black or African beauty. Her husband is quite attractive, I would have been shocked beyond belief if he were black knowing what I know about how black men view us.*

Thanks for saying you don't consider 'nappy' to be negative. However, it's amazing that we, as black people, even have to say that to each other, but we do because if not, we can be attacked by other black people who project their negativity about our natural hair onto whoever had the nerve to mention the word "nappy". LOL! Of course, "nappy" is not negative to everybody. It's just another *construct.* All constructs start out as opinions and pick up speed depending on the number of people who buy into them. "Nappy" hair is simply hair with a very tight curl. It's people who project their negativity onto nappy hair, and then they begin to think that their projection is shared by everyone.

LOL! Regarding black men not wanting Alec Wek, I think I read somewhere that one bm said he finds her very attractive. It's easy for him to say that, but I wonder whether he would strut around proudly with her on his arm.

Mon Jan 22, 10:27:00 AM EST

Halima said...

Evia, one of the reasons why I put a link to a picture of Clara Benjamin is to head off any assumption that when I said conventional beauty, I was speaking in terms of European norms.

Africans too have their conventional beauty, and if you ever asked an African man who has never met or come across a white person, nor seen any Hollywood movie, etc., I am sure they too have their 'ideal' for female beauty, which they have gleaned from the women around them. I can't prove anything but I do not know if Alec would be classed as beautiful by such black men.

Of course the whole issue of who is beautiful is so subjective anyway and vain, but for the sake of argument, let's say there is such a thing as female beauty (by whatever standards); I think Alec might be seen as a bit too masculine to fit that category.

Let me also add that the vast majority of us would be classed as average looking anyway, so no big deal!

Now I do not think it lets down my black dignity to suggest that Alec doesn't fall into the beautiful category. After all not every woman is and neither should we feel 'compelled' to say any African woman we see is wonderfully beautiful to 'beef up' our race.

Indeed the idea of beauty is expanding and that's very good, but on the whole, models are not even chosen for their beauty; they are chosen for their 'striking' body structure that can show off clothes. Alec has that to the max!

Mon Jan 22, 11:00:00 AM EST

Evia said..

> *I do not know if Alec would be classed as beautiful by such black men.*

Re what African men find beautiful, I do remember asking my ex (an African) about that and he said that African men—the ones less exposed to the western mindset—do not see beauty the way Europeans do. He said that to an African man, a woman's exterior beauty and desirability cannot be separated from her interior beauty because a woman, no matter how she looks on the outside, is not considered desirable *if* she has a nasty attitude and is unable to fit into her cultural role. So to them, if Beyonce has a nasty attitude, she would be good for sex, but they would never take her around other Africans.

Therefore, whatever "beauty" she has would be null and void as a criteria for a committed relationship.

I'm sure you're aware that many Africans are very culture and family-oriented. Traditionally and even these days, a typical African man cannot just choose a woman based on what he wants IF that woman won't fit into his culture or family or if she's really unacceptable to the family. So since facial beauty is not important or revered by some African cultures the way it is in the West, it is not focused on nearly to the extent it is here. In the past, the Africans who had had the most exposure to the West were the ones who were more likely to follow western ideals of beauty. Nowadays, with many Africans traveling to the west, living here for long periods, the export of western TV shows and movies via satellite, the western ideals are spreading fast throughout Africa and the rest of the world (for ex. skin bleaching by some African women and men.)

Insofar as body structure, I can say definitely that many African men like a woman with a full derriere—and even lots of non-black men do too—IF they have a choice. Many non-black men have not had that choice as much in the past.

If any one of us carefully and earnestly analyzes our view of black beauty, we'd really have to ask why it is that any black woman is not considered beautiful. We'd have to dissect Alec's face, for ex. and explain why this feature or that one is not beautiful. Similarly, what is so beautiful about Beyonce? I would guess that most people believe Beyonce is beautiful because they've been conditioned (by European beauty ideals) to think that a woman who looks more like Beyonce is more beautiful as opposed to Alec. It makes me wonder exactly how Alec would be viewed by a typical African person who'd never internalized European beauty ideals.

Sometimes, that can be so interesting, asking a person *why* they think a certain way. I've found that most people don't know why they think a certain way and this is why most people are so easily manipulated. Certain thoughts have been planted in our minds by others and we've internalized these thoughts, claimed them as our own without even thinking about whether they're healthy, productive thoughts or thoughts that are in our own best interests. I think there's an epidemic of that among black people.

Therefore, many black people don't, at this point, know which end is up and this is why many black women—since they're my

focus—keep working against our own best interests.
Mon Jan 22, 12:01:00 PM EST
Marlene said...

> *The real desire for equal rights—at least from a black male perspective—was to have equal access to white women without being lynched.*

I generally agree with many of the comments on this blog, but this statement is a gross assumption. This may have been what the fight was about for a few black men but not the other 97%. I believe this because although black men have greater and free access to white women (and other non-black women), only 3% marry out. Although, there is an increasing dislike for black women, I dare not believe that black men marched with their mothers and wives while being sprayed by water and attacked by dogs just to lay up with some white woman.

I do not think I will be in agreement with white racists that black men in general are immature, pale vagina-driven individuals.

However, I do believe many individuals in our society have reached a heightened state of selfishness and black males are no exception. The motto "get yourself the best and screw the rest" is rampant. The *best* to many black males is a light black female or/white. It's no secret. Oh well, their loss.

One reason why I believe black males have the beliefs that light or 'white is right' is because of family members and the other black males in their environment that they come into contact with. I remember I heard my little brother's friend on our front porch talking, and he said, *"When I grow up, I'm going to marry a white girl, what about you?"* I was shocked because they were only eight years old, and the question came out of nowhere.

Why did he say this? Well, because we lived in Colorado, where 30% of the black men are married to non-black women and our block had nothing but black males married to white women or very successful single black mothers.

So, you see they (black males) teach each other to have total and utter disdain for black women and that the beauty of a black woman is not to be desired. I heard black males teaching each other throughout my entire childhood, which one of the reason I decided to look over the fence (date interracially). Well actually someone was looking over the fence at me.

I just wanted to say, Evia, I love this blog! You are so intelligent, cultured, and open-minded. Thanks for putting your time and effort into this blog. I am married but I know there are a lot of black women who are single and need to hear what you are saying.

Chandra said...

Great article, very interesting, thought-provoking comments, arguments. Everyone, I'm sooo proud to see you discussing without *dissing*. I'm going to come out of lurk and join in these discussions more often.

Mon Jan 22, 04:36:00 PM EST

Meli said...

I can't tell you how ego boosting that sidebar featuring those couples (ex and current) has been. I also had no idea Alec Wek was even married, yet alone to a non-black man. I imagine him to be tall. He is also very handsome. I have never heard Alec Wek speak, but looking at the photo above in which she is smiling and looking more human instead of that fierce look on the runway (that models are trained to display), she looks softer and more real to life. If she were a talk show host, folks would likely warm up to her because that gives her life and a personality. Otherwise, narrow-minded people still see an "odd" looking BW—because she is not what we are used to seeing especially in high fashion.

Evia made a good point about the "construct" of beauty also. I feel that whatever society places a high premium on is what we will find desirable. If all of a sudden small feet became a symbol of femininity, women everywhere would have bones removed, shortened, and everything. We fall prey to anything and any passing notion stating that we could be better if only...

BW just have not chosen to stop being victims yet of our own negative stuff, not even the stuff that others put on us. Of all the circumstances we cannot change, like disease, we *can* change our attitudes toward others and accept love from other men.

Mon Jan 22, 05:02:00 PM EST

Ann said...

> *I am always happy to see another black woman with short nappy hair (I don't consider "nappy" to be a negative way to describe our hair).*

For a good discussion on the good hair-bad hair dichotomy, visit this link:

http://www.rachelstavern.com/?p=304

Mon Jan 22, 06:10:00 PM EST

Tom said...

I've been reading through your blog for the past couple of weeks and started with the first one listed. There are quite a few things I want to comment on, so please bear with the flood.

First, a little history: I am a white man married to a black woman, and we've been married just over a year. I grew up in an all-white town and began dating outside of my race in the middle of serving four years in the Army, but I did not date a black woman until 1999 while working for a popular Internet travel agency. She was a former flight attendant and was even the winner of Mrs. San Diego even though she was divorced at the time. Her lineage was Ethiopian. She did teach me a ton about what black people go through, and I would usually tell her she's making a big thing by calling something racist when I thought it was insignificant, like someone touching her wig. Unfortunately, she suffered from bi-polar disorder and had extreme, sometimes violent, mood swings.

I also got burned by a true AA gold digger (Quote: "Money covers a multitude of sins!") that had a proud history of bedding married men, and a scammer from Africa (she was married but told several guys she wanted to meet them, and managed to talk money out of each of us). I've learned many lessons, good and bad. Thankfully, I found my wife from California and she agreed to move to Texas where we are now building a life together. She and I both work for a better life, and we are getting there.

I did grow up in a Christian home, but it was tinged with some racism from one side of the family. Using the N-word was forbidden but we never interacted with other races, except for a select few families. Our family worked hard and we came to expect that in our spouses.

It has been quite an experience learning how to interact with a different culture yet keep my own. There can be clashes, usually humorous. I get picked on because I don't barbecue very well, but "like iron sharpens iron," we all grow.

Evia, some of the things in your blog I agree with. I do agree that people are responsible for their own actions. Looking from the outside in, I shake my head wondering when black men are going to quit trying to pull other black men down and start pushing each other to be better. Yes, I know there is still a prominent undercurrent of racism that does pull some down, but not everyone is going to be caught up in it. Others will use that as an excuse to underachieve. Of all the lessons to learn from white men, why not cultivate more emphasis on becoming educated with less infighting? If a person gives up without giving a full fight against pressures and temptations, that person does give power to whomever or whatever else blows in one day and out the next, almost a voluntary submission. I cheer when I learn of a successful black family, especially when they turn around and pull others along with them. That, to me, is extreme success!

There was some talk about 'gold diggers', princesses, and marrying up. I honestly consider myself blessed since my background taught me to look beyond dollar signs and "stuff" in general to see a person for who they are.

Evia, I take a little umbrage to the idea that a black woman must *marry up*, that a man who struggles isn't worth a black woman's time. I would agree that a man who isn't trying to make a better life and is willing to live off others is a leech and isn't worth the clothes on his back. However, an honest man that is ready to treat a woman right and is able to provide a safe home and is going to protect it all, that should be the key. Or he should be okay if he is struggling to move forward instead of simply struggling, flopping around in the same muck without any effort to do anything else. I personally wouldn't want a spouse that isn't willing to work, whether it be a job or at home, because I work hard. We both have our lazy times, though. On the flip side, I want to give my wife gifts when I can. I love it when she does those girly things that make her feel good because she smiles. She doesn't demand them, and it makes it that much sweeter to see her happy when she gets a gift or splurges.

Evia, you had mentioned that you wish black men would look past the exterior (I think you were talking about skin color and some body shape). In the same manner, I hope some women learn to look past the $$ and straight into the man's heart. No, there's nothing wrong with wanting to be comfortable, but marriage cannot be turned into a business transaction.

I mentioned skin color. My own preference is darker is more attractive in my eyes. I don't know exactly why, but part of it stems from my background. I am attracted to differences. I want to be, and to have difference. I love to see the contrast between white and black skin hand-in-hand. I love the depth in dark skin. Yes, ok, I also like an endowed derrière, I'll admit it. LOL! "Difference" is more exciting and richer because each person brings a different viewpoint. Even if both agree, each person will have a different reason why. It forces each person to question their own beliefs and, hopefully, change them when they are wrong.

Concerning the Duke Rape case, I honestly believe her race was (or should have been) secondary. Why? White people have always had a history of vilifying women in the adult entertainment industry. It's only been recently that a change in thinking has taken place where any woman has a right to say "no" and it be respected. This doesn't mean there was no racism in how the Duke case was handled, but I know that kind of thinking (she was an exotic dancer) has extended from whites to other white people for centuries past.

There is an interesting change of generations happening now. Many of the people that lived through the Civil Rights movement are beginning to retire or pass away. Although racism still exists, I believe it is waning slowly with fewer outbursts. What I'm hoping for are two additional things: no more reverse racism and no more in-fighting. I don't believe that the N-word should be used between black people since it is a derogatory word. No amount of twisted logic could convince me otherwise. Also, if "race relations" are to move forward, white people must continue to admit the crimes of the past but cease the racism, and black people cannot use that past as an excuse to indulge in reverse racism. Conflicts will happen. Deal with each one without condemning an entire race.

Anyway, that's all I can blather on my soapbox. I like your message that black women should open the gate and see honest white men as potential. I also like that you are shedding light on the differences between the two races and how it all can harmonize in a relationship, though I'd love to see more of that. I like that you are sending a message to black women to think more highly of themselves and go for what they need in a man, and no settling! I like the message that a black woman doesn't have to be on guard with everyone anymore, and she doesn't have to meet any interaction with instant defense.

I look forward to more posts!

Mon Jan 22, 06:11:00 PM EST
Las said...

> *"Thanks for saying you don't consider 'nappy' to be negative. However, it's amazing that we, as black people, even have to say that to each other, but we do because if not, we can be attacked by other black people who project their negativity about nappiness onto whoever had the nerve to mention the word "nappy". LOL!*

Hi Evia, I won't consider or describe my natural hair texture as "nappy". If someone wants to consider having "naps" to describe their hair or the hair texture on top of their newborn's head, then that's their prerogative. But don't think it's a "negative projection" if others don't accept it as the proper term for themselves. It's more of a term of preference.

@Evia re:

> *Of course, "nappy" is not negative.*

People who also use the word "mulatto" don't see it as negative either. They're both derived from the same "negative" projection towards us as black people. I also wonder for those that don't consider "nappy" as negative, would they honestly appreciate a White female stranger walking up to them and saying "wow look at your nappy hair today".

@ Anonymous:

> *The real desire for equal rights— at least from a black male perspective— was to have equal access to white women without being lynched.*

I agree. This is a fundamental revelation to understanding the discrepancy between black men and black women ideology. Growing up, I've always heard people say that some black men would be quite be satisfied as long as they can have a White woman and a White Cadillac. To heck with everything else. We see this all the time, even in our generation in many ways and forms.

Mon Jan 22, 06:24:00 PM EST

Evia said...

Welcome, Marlene! Thank you for all of your comments.

> *I believe this because although black men have greater and free access to white women (and other non-blacks) only 3% marry-out.*

Actually according to the 2000 U.S. Census, 9.7% of black men were married to non-black women. That number has certainly risen since 2000. And according to Michael Eric Dyson's statistics, in some states like California and several others, 20% or more of bm are married to non-black women. According to Dyson, a relatively large percentage of black male college graduates, black men with professional degrees, and black men who earn more than $60,000 a year are married to non-black women. Since African American women are overwhelmingly conditioned to *only* mate and marry men in their ethnic group, accurate statistics are critical to this discussion. Upwardly-mobile black women need to know that they have to exercise their option to date and marry out IF they plan to be 'equally yoked.' If I were a single black woman, I would want the most accurate statistics. I will post these statistics and links to them soon or if anyone else has them handy, please go ahead and send them to me and I'll post them. We have to have accurate info because many people, especially, some black men will try to minimize these figures in order to cloak what their brethren are doing.

Mon Jan 22, 07:02:00 PM EST

Ms CPA said...

Las, I take it your comment about a white person saying *"wow, look at your nappy hair"* is directed in part at me. So, first I'll say I feel good about myself and the, yes, nappy hair on my head, so, to answer your hypothetical question, if anyone (stranger or not) were to make that type of comment to me, I would assume they were complimenting me, and would say *"why, thank you."* It takes a rather mean-spirited person to say I wasn't complimenting you, but if they did, I would just say, *"I like my hair the way it is, thank you very much"* and move on.

Mon Jan 22, 07:06:00 PM EST

Evia said...

Also, Marlene, let me add that my statistics above only pertain to the black men who "married" non-black women. There are many black men these days who exclude black women from their "dating" pool *or* only date black women sometimes. Do those black women also date non-black men sometimes? Mostly, they don't and this means that they're not usually dating anyone when the black guy is dating others. Additionally, there are some black men who are shacking up with non-black women, white women mainly. So overall, there are many black men who are not available to black women at any point in time and the Census does not reflect all of this and instead only reflects the marriages.

Mon Jan 22, 07:24:00 PM EST
Evia said...

I'm watching "Lincoln Heights" a series on the ABC Family Channel that features an IR relationship between the black teenage daughter and a white guy. The relationship is regarded in a refreshing way by her family. She's gotten some of the usual reactions from some of her black peers though, but she's strong enough to brush them off. Check it out if you can get this channel.

Mon Jan 22, 07:29:00 PM EST
Evia said...

Welcome, Chandra and thank you! Please come out of lurk mode again and soon.

Mon Jan 22, 07:36:00 PM EST
Evia said...

Tom, Welcome to you too! Wow, you had been saving it up. That's great. We love folks who have a lot to say here, so feel free.

Yep, scam artists are out there and they come in all skin shades, ethnicities, nationalities, and genders.

> *Evia, I take a little umbrage to the idea that a black woman must marry up, that a man who struggles isn't worth a black woman's time. I would agree that a man who isn't trying to make a better life and is willing to live off others is a leech and isn't worth the clothes on his back. However, an honest man that is ready to treat a woman right and is able to provide a safe home and is going to protect it all, that should be the key. If he is struggling to move forward instead of simply struggling, flopping around*

> *in the same muck without any effort to do anything else...I personally wouldn't want a spouse that isn't willing to work, whether it be a job or at home, because I work hard.*

Tom, I certainly don't think any woman should marry "down." At the least, she should marry someone at her level, however, I hear what you're saying. I'm a capable and generous woman in many ways. I also bring a lot to a relationship, and I have to have a man who brings a lot also. I'm a firm believer in being 'equally yoked.' I can appreciate a man who is struggling, but I've always made enough money to support myself very well. I wouldn't want to meet a man and start struggling with him when I wasn't struggling *before* I met him.

This also depends on various factors. If a man is struggling when he's 28, that's one thing, but if he's 'struggling' when he's 38, 48, or 58, that's something else. Since I invested my time and energy very early in my life to avoid all of this struggling, I wouldn't want the man in my life to bring me to the point of struggling. If Darren were to leave me today, I would be financially fine because I can support myself very well—all by myself.

Mon Jan 22, 08:10:00 PM EST

Evia said...

> *I also wonder for those that don't consider "nappy" as negative, would honestly appreciate a White female stranger walking up to them and saying "wow look at your nappy hair today.*

Of course, it would all depend on how she said it because tone of voice and facial expression can totally change the meaning of the most innocent words, however, I wouldn't have a problem with a white person saying my hair is "nappy" because it is. Nappy to me means hair with "a very tight curl." That, to me, would be the same as me saying to a redhead, "*Wow, look at your red hair today.*" Nappy hair is the same as straight hair or any other kind of hair to me. It's no better or worse, regardless of whether tons of other people have issues about it or not. Those are *their* issues; not mine.

Mon Jan 22, 08:21:00 PM EST

Ann said...

> ["Beauty is very trend-oriented, thus subjective. What is beautiful today was considered ugly yesterday. We fit the mold, come close to fitting the mold, or are not even considered worthy of a mold. We live in a culture where ideal beauty is personified in a White, blue-eyed blond slim woman with surgically altered proportions. The closer we are to this ideal, the more acceptance we receive."
>
> "And no one receives more alienation in the race to beauty than black women."
>
> "Black women aren't spiteful over seeing white women with black men. They are sick of seeing images of white women as the dominant standard of desirability."
>
> "White men have immense power in labeling and, thus, legitimizing female desirability. A white man can date a pretty woman from any racial or ethnic group and tell the world to accept the goodness of her beauty simply because he picked her. For example, at one time dating Asian women was unacceptable because their beauty wasn't white enough. When an increasing number of white men "discovered" Asian beauty, they became a non-controversial choice for white men. Then it became safe to allow white women to date Asian men."]

SOURCE: *Big Little White Lies: Our Attempt to White-out America,* by Carol Chehade. Nehmarche Publishing, Inc. 2001.

Mon Jan 22, 08:27:00 PM EST

Las said...

I just posted a comment a second ago and I don't know where it went.

Ms CPA, I'm sorry if I offended you. It was not meant that way. I never thought about it before, but I would prefer terms like: *tight curls, exotic curls* (only because they're different to society), *beauty curls, soft curls, beauty tress, natural tress,* etc. I know these sounds corny but I'm sure after I post this, better terms will come to mind.

I went on that website link that Ann put up. I didn't finish reading all the comments. There was talk about black women straightening their hair as a form of being somewhat compliant to White beauty standards. I don't agree to that for everyone these days, per se. Another thing is that ancient Egyptian women (they were black women that looked different from the ones there now) *straightened* their hair as a form of style. They did not emulate anyone's straight hair standards. It was their own imagination and creation. I personally love my hair straight. I don't wear weaves and I keep my hair very long (jet-black) and pass the mid of my back. In high school and even now, I get a lot of attention from it, both good and bad. I feel feminine and beautiful with it like this. Maybe our society has me feeling that way. I'm willing to admit that.

I admire small dreads or "locks" but they are not for me at this time, and I won't follow the religious aspect of it either way. Even so, society still has its bias limitations for someone who is not established career-wise before they make that statement. Unfortunately. Even so, it got me thinking. In regard to the sentiments on this particular blog, how many white males are honestly receptive to black women who have short "nappy" hair. I'm sure there are a few. But apart from my own belief, how many would really consider us if our hair was locked, "nappy" or short and "nappy?"

Mon Jan 22, 08:31:00 PM EST

Ann said...

Las, at that site, the discussion centered on how people consider black women's hair as less than beautiful, if it is nappy. I personally love my nappy hair. And I do not consider myself as less than desirable because I do not straighten my hair. Straight is not for me. Our hair is unique; no other race in the world has the gravity-defying hair that we black people have, and the very thought of me altering my hair with a perm makes me feel less than what I am.

Wear your hair the way you want to. In the end, it's important to me, the way I feel about black women and their hair. Straighten mine after white America has denigrated, debased, and vilified black women's features, especially our hair? No.

Our hair is not naturally straight (unless we have more non-black racial admixture in us to cause our hair to not be nappy). So, for me to chemically alter my hair is to be ashamed of what I have. (I mean me, not you, Las.) And I am not ashamed of my beautiful, tightly-coiled, kinky, "nappy" hair.

Mon Jan 22, 08:49:00 PM EST

Ann said...

> People who also use the word "mulatto" don't see it as negative either.

People who have no problem with the word "mulatto" should. It is a degrading insult from the days of slavery/miscegenation, under the belief that children of slave masters and black slave women were akin to being like mules, and therefore, like mules, sterile, and unable to reproduce themselves.

—Mulatto, according to Merriam-Webster's:

[Sp. mulato, fr. mulo [mule], fr. L mulus] (1593) 1. the first generation offspring of a black person and a white person. 2. a person of mixed white and black ancestry. So, this term is racist, and insulting.

Why anyone currently would still continue to use such a debasing term is beyond me.

Mon Jan 22, 09:08:00 PM EST

Stacy Jones said...

@ Miss CPA

You are very right about the use of models lacking conventional beauty. There are a number of white models (google Gemma Ward and Kate Moss). Liya Kebede is also another black African model who has done very well in the business.

Mon Jan 22, 09:35:00 PM EST

Ms CPA said...

No offense taken, Las. I enjoy reading opinions that aren't the same as mine and would be bored if we all felt the same way about everything

Mon Jan 22, 10:17:00 PM EST

Anonymous said...

I know this sounds awful, but I have a confession to make. If I had a choice I would rather be of a fair complexion. However, my most unattractive feature is my nose—large, flared nostrils and flat tip.

I often wished I had done plastic surgery in my younger days. I would often stand before the mirror, pinch my nose together, and imagine what I'd look like if my features were different and how confident and beautiful I would feel, "if" only, etc.

As a young child growing up, my family and distant relatives would often tease me and make awful comments about my nose and in doing so, have brainwashed me so terribly about my features, that, even now, as an adult, I still struggle terribly with this issue.

Contrary to what some say about white society's standards of beauty imposed upon blacks, I must honestly confess that for me, it was my black family and relatives who instilled this terrible form of self-hate in me, not "white" society.

I wish I had the confidence of others like the model Alec, but I don't. I know I need to accept the features I was born with, but maybe it's too late; perhaps the damage is already done? I am guessing that there may be a few others out there who feel as I do but are too shy and afraid of persecution from the black community to voice it.

Mon Jan 22, 10:36:00 PM EST

Marlene said...

My apologies Evia, the percentage I gave was incorrect. I thought it seemed low when my professor said it in class. She did say her data was old, so I should have definitely checked for myself before I posted. Thanks.

Mon Jan 22, 10:58:00 PM EST

Evia said...

I think there are so many misconceptions about what does and does not attract white men to black women.

@Las:

Please don't take offense at my questions that follow, but I'm trying to get a handle on how some black women think about some of these aspects of the IR realm, the black-white attraction and so forth, etc. This is an opportunity for all of us to learn more about each other and to learn more about various aspects, so I'd like to ask you a couple of questions, but keep in mind that my questions regarding white men only pertain to those white men who are interested in black women.

Here goes: You've talked about hair and brought up the issue of white men and black women's hair. My questions to you are:

1. Do you realize that white men know that black women have nappy hair or at least, they know that the hair of a typical black woman is not euro hair? Or do you think that they think that our hair is the same or almost the same as euro hair? From some of your

comments, it seems that you think that hair is important to white men, to some extent, for ex. the texture, length, etc. of black women's hair, so my question re this is:

2. IF a woman's hair length and straightness (or non-nappiness) is a biggie with these men, why do you think that the ones who are interested in black women would be interested in us?

About my hair—

When I started dating white males, I was wearing my hair in big braids. Then I wore cornrows and then I went to small micro braids (synthetic additions) but anyone could see that my natural hair was kinky/nappy. I hadn't straightened my hair in about 10 years. I just assumed that if a white male was interested in me, he also liked my nappy hair and that if he wanted/preferred someone with straight hair, he would have just been with a white/Asian, etc. woman.

IMO, people—who think that nappy hair is less-than hair—have "issues" because nappy or tightly coiled hair is just another type of natural hair. I feel the same about people who don't like straight hair. The thing is that I don't take other peoples' issues on myself. So if a straight-haired person or anyone doesn't like my nappy hair, they need to work on themselves—or their issues because my hair is fine and just as great as anyone else's. This is what I project because this is what I believe.

By the time I met Darren, I was still wearing my hair in micro-braids. Soon after meeting him, it was time for me to get my braids re-done, so I asked him to help me to take them out, and he did. I wanted him to see my natural hair. I wore my hair in the micro braids for a few years after we got married, but I decided at a certain point to go totally natural and just wear my hair with no synthetic stuff added.

This has morphed into a get-up-and-go, natural, 2-stranded twist hairstyle now. As can be expected, it is always a non-black man who will compliment my hairstyle or I'll see one of them looking at my hair and I figure they like my natural look or find something unique or "exotic" about it.

Mon Jan 22, 11:32:00 PM EST
Marlene said...

Contrary to what some say about white society's standards of beauty imposed upon blacks, I must

> *honestly confess that for me, it was my black family and relatives who instilled this terrible form of self-hate in me, not "white" society.*

Any negative comments I have ever heard about black features, skin color, and hair were all from relatives, friends of the family, and other black people in my environment, not whites. I have heard and seen pictures of how white people used to denigrate the physical attributes of blacks but I have not witnessed it personally in my life.

I am not saying whites don't still put down typical black characteristics. I will say that I think blacks continue to pass from generation to generation their shame and hatred of being black. Blacks may have learned to hate self from whites, but we have not needed their help in continuing to do so.

Mon Jan 22, 11:42:00 PM EST
Evia said...

> *I know this sounds awful but I have a confession to make.*

Hello Anonymous and Welcome! It took courage to make your confession. It's good though to just come out and say it—share it with others of us. Don't feel that you are alone because you're not. Many black people feel the same way you do about either their hair, complexion, nose, lips, etc. or their entire selves. Also, many women of other races and ethnicities feel the same way. Yet, as you say, it was not whites who taught you not to like your complexion and nose, it was your own people—black people.

Now I hope no one comes up with the excuse:

> *Well, white folks taught us to hate ourselves!*

(SMH) Adults must take responsibility for changing their own destructive thinking and behavior. Why aren't more black folks saying this and pressuring each other to change? Sometimes, I feel like such a lone voice. Why don't prominent black males tell other black males to stop chasing after light-bright-white women because it clearly shows their self-hate. Blacks should know that many whites understand that. If there were just a few prominent black men selecting out whiter-skinned, white wives, or non-black wives/mates, that would be different. However, when this is such a widespread phenomenon, it's a pattern, and it indicates a lack of appreciation of blacks and instead: idolatry of whites.

Anyway, let me ask you, what do you think would have to happen at this point to make you feel better about yourself, accept yourself?

Tue Jan 23, 12:05:00 AM EST
Halima said...

> One of the reasons why this reality is not openly discussed in the black community IMO is because it in essence proves that what racist whites have been saying for centuries is correct. The real desire for equal rights—at least from a black male perspective—was to have equal access to white women without being lynched. Noting more. It was not about uplifting and helping the community as a whole take advantage of the hard earned opportunities.

I think what we are really getting at here is changing in 'class'-type interests. When you are bound in a certain class, your zeal for improvement of that class is highest. You will have no problems going on protest marches and doing 'sit ins,' etc. However once class doors are open, your interests are likely to 'mutate'. This is also the same with status groups (different races). Once there are opportunities to escape the consequences of being a particular race, the need to 'stand shoulder to shoulder' with each other is weakened.

Many of us expected that being black, black interests would continue to 'trump' every other concern, but with bm, we are beginning to see that this isn't the case and that once the more serious penalties for being black are removed or lessened (lynching), they are and will move on to 'other' preoccupations and a more self-serving agenda. Therefore, bm sharing mainstream values and pursuits needn't fill us with surprise. It's just a normal progression, which we failed to or refused to take into account when we drew up our strategies for black emancipation!

This was a gross miscalculation within black activism because anyone who has read a bit of Marx and Webber knows that class/status interest can shift. This calls for a redefinition of the terms/basis of black activism, i.e., we need to revisit and update our understanding of the reason why any black person would want to engage in an overarching struggle today.

I also forget to add that I wish Alec and her handsome beau all the very best and may they have scores of children.

http://dateawhiteguy.blogspot.com/

Tue Jan 23, 06:03:00 AM EST

Las said...

Evia, LOL. I am well aware that white people know black people generally have *natural* curls. However, knowing and accepting are two different things. I don't know what is desired by white men. That's why I asked the question. Perhaps if I see more white men with black women who look more "afro-centric," then I wouldn't have to ask. White men can admire, but will they generally accept? Then again, you Evia might say afro-centric women don't want these men.

I am very pro-black and pro-femininity, but I mentioned my hair the way it is for a reason. You, being a woman with natural hair, not knowing that, would you have a certain perception of what kind of oriented thinking black woman I am because of how I keep mine?

I realize that I may also have a little cultural difference next to you and some of the others here. Even so, I grew up hearing "*a woman's hair is her beauty.*" I'm a firm believer of that. It can be straight, locked, braided, cut up, natural curls, etc. It's all beautiful to the individual wearing it or the eye of the beholder. I keep mine the way it is because I like it—me. It seems it's a way of life for most black women and me in this era. It was done to my hair when I was in my early teens like picking out a training bra. it had nothing to do with looking like a white woman or trying to look like a woman a white man would want, (not that I'm saying you're implying that).

I'm thinking about putting in neat locs in the future, but I have to get situated with my career first. This is important to me. People still discriminate against locs. Sad.

Tue Jan 23, 08:28:00 AM EST

Evia said...

> *I think what we are really getting at here is changing in 'class-'type interests.*
>
> *When you are bound in a certain class, your zeal for improvement of that class is highest. You will have no problems going on protest marches and*

> *doing 'sit ins' etc. However once class doors are open, your interests are likely to 'mutate.'*

Halima, thanks for the 'class' perspective. In the U.S., the issue of 'class' is downplayed. It's one of those issues that's almost taboo to talk about, yet it's a biggie whenever we talk about people because obviously people do come from different social and economic classes. I certainly agree that different social and economic classes of people tend to look out for their own interests.

However, many black people (including many bm with white mates) would declare that there is only one class for *all* black people and that's the "black" class. LOL! They would point out that this is how white America and white supremacist structures view us; therefore this is what we are. Many AAs absolutely see themselves through "white eyes" and through racist white eyes only.

Let's face it. Most black people cannot even conceive of defining themselves and if you can't define yourself, then you're using someone else's definition of you. Furthermore, if you can't define yourself or have the wrong definition of who you are, then you can't possibly see what's in your best interest. Whew! When I've pointed out on occasion that I define myself in all the key ways, I get black people who want to attack me! Yet, accepting the false definition of others is clearly why so many black people, and specifically black women agonize over how we look. This is what holds us back from strutting out there to get the best loving and most loveable man we can find.

This is why so many black women cannot believe that a white man with an enlightened mindset can look at a black woman and see the beauty in her dark skin, and non-euro facial features and hair, and want to love her and share his life with her and want her to be the mother of his children.

Anyway, since many blacks see themselves and others as being confined to the "black class," they hate it when they see any black person act like they're not in that class or when they see another black person try to escape the confinement. Confinement is oppressive—period. No one wants to be confined, restricted, suppressed, stuck with no or few options, etc., but some people are too afraid to try to escape.

Escaping doesn't mean mating and marrying non-blacks. Escaping to me means *'living well,'* having many choices, and the means to actualize those choices irrespective of the skin-shade or ethnicity of your social circle or mate. For ex., I 'lived well' with my ex-husband, an African man. My life with him—here and in Nigeria—enabled me to have a type of life that very few AA women can even imagine. In Nigeria, I mingled with 'la crème de la crème' of Nigerian society and with wealthy European expatriates and visiting dignitaries. I also lived well in this country with him. That was our lifestyle because of his profession; he's good at what he does.

I've considered that some black men who date and marry out are exercising their right to define themselves as simply a man who sees a woman who appeals to him for whatever reason. In other words, I don't think that *all* black men who date and marry out are self-haters. I would support these men except that a great proportion of them do seem to be with non-black women of lower quality or of significantly lesser quality than they would require if the woman were black. They lower the bar for non-black women. That's rotten; that's discriminatory. For ex., in my travels, I often see bm with very overweight, even obese ww, whereas many bm say loudly these days that they don't date bw because so many bw are overweight. My thirtyish bm cousin also says that he hears bm say flatly that a bw has to meet stricter criteria, bring more to their table than they would ask from a non-black woman. That's *racial* discrimination.

When upwardly mobile black women mate or marry non-black men, these men are rarely ever considered of lower quality by whites, blacks, or anyone. Also many interracially married or interracially involved bm tend to devalue or denigrate all bw and the wealthy ones (doctors, lawyers, business executives, the intelligentsia, entertainers, professional athletes, etc.) take their resources into other communities. This latter group is of particular concern since these resource-rich (in terms of influence, education, talent, skills, money, etc.) ones of them who marry out are taking badly-needed resources that the black community (including many black women) have paved the way for them to get.

Have you noticed that bm who are ex-inmates, drug abusers, permanently unemployed, uneducated, serially homeless, impoverished and other similar ones are not the ones or are very seldom among the ones who mate or marry out? This is not surprising because without money or the means to make a productive living, non-black women don't want those men, just like black women don't.

Upwardly mobile black women, however, are loudly criticized by bm for not "rescuing" or "repairing" broken bm, whereas neither upwardly mobile nor any other type of white woman, Asian woman, etc. is ever expected to pick up and repair a broke-down bm.

Yet, the many non-black women who vie for the attention of upscale bm are, to my knowledge, never labeled *golddiggers* by wealthy or well-positioned bm, whereas many times, black women—who even ask whether a bm has a job—are considered to be interested in him for his money, or accused of being a *gold digger*. I also must point out what many bm overlook for some reason: black women *do* know that many black men don't really have substantial monetary resources or any gold to "dig," so if that were a bw's main reason for being interested in a black man, she'd really be out of luck. She'd instead *almost always* look at white or whiter men. So that's a ludicrous and foul accusation for bm to make. The fact is that in 2008, bw still overwhelmingly gravitate towards black men—job or no job, and this puts the woman in a minus position.

Many bm in the resource-rich category don't often publicly acknowledge the tremendous unconditional support they enjoy from black women. It was/is black folks, including many black women, who knocked down the doors for them to get those resources and it's black women who support them the most. Yet, when they make public statements about black women, often these statements are derogatory (Wesley Snipes, OJ, Arsenio Hall, etc.) and widely broadcasted.

However, I've noticed that when/if IR-married black men have any racially motivated experience (criticism, discrimination, negative interaction with law officials, etc.) they always play their "black card" like Clarence Thomas and OJ did. At that point, they always seem to remember that bw can and do have something of quality to offer—loyalty and support. This is why I beg black women not to support them in any way when they try to play that card because they don't reciprocate. People do not respect you when they can mistreat you and still get support from you

So, yes, I've married Darren, but I've never removed myself from the black community. He also contributes his resources (time, energy, skills, information, etc.) to the black community on an ongoing basis. I also have stated that, prior to meeting and marrying Darren, I most definitely included black men in my dating pool because I know that quality men come in all skin shades. No one will ever find any indication that I ever discriminated against bm based on skin shade or hair texture or stereotypic African features or traits.

So, there are a lot of AA men, for sure, in the discriminators' category and they are increasing. This is another reason why I continue this blog. My blog is sort of like an 'equalizer'—not to get back at those black men, but because as Pearl Jr. says: "Black Women Need Love Too!" I would love it if black women would focus *only* on the men of the world who accept bw in all of our African-descended glorious beauty.

Tue Jan 23, 08:36:00 AM EST
Evia said...

> *I am well aware that white people know black people generally have natural curls. However, knowing and accepting are two different things.*

Las, maybe I'm not understanding you, but I firmly believe that any white man who's interested in dating a black woman *accepts* that our hair is different and doesn't care. It might even be one of the reasons he's interested, except if he says that, he can be accused of having a fetish. LOL! As you know, the area of white-black attraction is loaded with land mines! People on neither side feel free to talk about what appeals to them about that person of a different race—especially whites and blacks.

Darren loves to sink his fingers into my spongy, nappy hair but told me that he wouldn't have ever told me that in the beginning because he wasn't sure how I'd react. Darren, as well as other white men I've talked with have stated that they think that black women straighten their hair or wear weaves to get a 'different look or style,' just like wearing a new outfit. They know that the permed straight or blond hair is not *our* hair. Some of them know that some black women are trying to get a "white" look. It's just not something they think about much because it's not that important to them. I really don't think that most men care much about why you're with them; they're just glad you're with them. I think it's women who like to analyze why a man is with them and whether he really, really loves her or whether he totally thinks she's hot. LOL!

Also, from what I've read, heard, experienced, and observed, white people don't think about hair texture, length, etc. the *same* way black people do. They don't fixate on it or spend nearly the time, energy, or money on it the way blacks do. That is, except for bald or balding white people like Donald Trump.

> *I don't know what on earth is desired by White men, that's why I asked the question.*

Las, I'm not going to be able to answer all of your questions about what white men desire. Have you ever considered just walking over to a suitable white man in a safe setting, and just having a conversation with him, since you have this amount of curiosity about them? I think this is one of the things more black women need to start doing. If this is done in the right way, it can enlarge your world so much! I'm not saying you should use this as a 'pick up' tactic, but just as a way of getting more information. The man will most likely be very flattered that you chose him to answer your questions.

> *Perhaps if I see more White men with black women who look more "afro-centric,*

It's not clear what you mean by "afro-centric." As I travel around, I see plenty of white men with black women who wear locs and twists these days and these women are of all complexions. Could you be more specific? Most of the black women with their white significant others in my sidebar photos look afro-centric and like typical AA women to me, if that's what you mean. Just because they're wearing a bunch of makeup, have their hair all done up and are dressed fancy doesn't mean they don't look "black." Yes, clearly some of them are very mixed or biracial, but I'd bet if you saw the majority of them out of the limelight like at the grocery store or at the mall, you'd see they look just like most of the rest of us.

One of the main reasons why I was hesitant to include "mixed" looking or biracial women in the sidebar is because I knew that many black women would focus on them and think that's why the white man wanted to be with them—because of their light skin and such.

> *White men can admire, but will they generally accept? Then again, you Evia might say afro-centric women don't want these men.*

Las, are you talking about black women with a 'black nationalist' mindset? Is that what you mean by "afro-centric?" Also I still don't understand what you mean by "accept."

> *I am very pro-black and pro-femininity, but I mentioned my hair the way it is for a reason. You, being a woman with natural hair, not knowing that would you have a certain perception of what kind of oriented thinking black woman I am because of how I keep mine?*

Not that you would know this, but I don't think that hair defines a person. I judge people by how they think which is reflected by what they say and mainly 'do.' You can make a big mistake judging a black woman by her hairstyle.

Tue Jan 23, 09:24:00 AM EST
Tom said . . .

> *I wouldn't want to meet a man and start 'struggling' with him when I wasn't 'struggling' before I met him. This also depends on various factors. If a man is 'struggling' when he's 28, that's one thing, but if he's 'struggling' when he's 38, 48, or 58, that's something else.*

Yes, I can appreciate that. By the time someone is in his mid-30s, something is going on. In my own history, siblings had to pay their own way through college. By my second year in 1992, I had run out of funds. Working full time and going to school full time had made the commute to school dangerous since I was falling asleep driving! I ended up joining the Army for 4 years but still had debt after leaving and didn't get back to it until recently.

Having grown up in a family that didn't have much but did have a good name, it makes me cringe when anyone puts so much emphasis on "stuff" instead of people. Please take my stance with a grain of salt since I was burned by a true gold digger.

Tue Jan 23, 09:58:00 AM EST
Evia said...

Tom, on the money front, I expect a man to prepare himself to provide and protect his family or have a plan that he's working hard to implement in order to provide and protect a family, and you did that from what you said. It doesn't mean that things are always going to work out according to plan, but if the first plan doesn't work, a man should put his 2nd plan into operation because surely he has a backup plan and even another one if that one fails! I don't expect him to say to me, "Well, it's easier for you to make money, so I'll just live off you."

Many people don't realize that there is a sizeable number (and growing) of AA men these days who think that way. They are actively searching for a woman to support them. This is how they make their living—going from woman to woman and living off these women—whether the woman is black, white, Hispanic, it doesn't matter to them. I've read that some white women these days feel sorry for, have guilt about racism and such, or are looking for a *Mandingo* stud black man, and they support these men or become their "sugarmomma." Many black women do too, but some black women refuse to do it, and *demand* that the men get a job or get more education, training, bring home money, and behave like real *men*, and this is when many of these men turn on black women and call us golddiggers and other denigrating names.

Tue Jan 23, 11:18:00 AM EST
Evia said...

Back to Alec Wek, here's a link below to an old article about Alec Wek that Felicia sent.

> *Ask her about her boyfriends and she clams up. Leonardo DiCaprio once introduced himself to her backstage at a show but she was not interested.*

http://www.findarticles.com/p/articles/mi_qn4153/is_200303 26/ai_n12038046

Carria said...

Marrying a white man will make neither his inherent skin privilege—nor the mentality to which it is attached—magically disappear. Tom articulated that perfectly in his posts when he talked about this contrived notion of 'reverse racism.' I would never feel comfortable being in a relationship with a white man, with a Tom.

And I certainly can't understand the obsession with mating solely with these men when there are a variety of other races to choose from if you're a black woman with no agenda other than love or looking to explore her relationship options. What makes them (white men) alone so special? Hopefully not the very "thing" that black men are being maligned ad nauseum about or are accused of pursuing.

It is peculiar to advocate black woman "broadening" (beyond black men) their dating scope...to just one other race of men.

Fri Jan 26, 12:06:00 PM EST

Evia said...

> Marrying a white man will make neither his inherent skin privilege—nor the mentality to which it is attached—magically disappear. Tom has articulated this perfectly in his posts.

I've certainly never said that marrying a white man would make his skin privileges or a racist mentality disappear. I've never advocated that black women get involved with racist white men in the first place, or with any type of small-minded man of any race, for that matter. I have advocated black women broaden their dating and marriage pool to include non-black men and non-African American men on numerous occasions throughout my blogs. I had a wonderful marriage to a continental African man at one point, so I certainly wouldn't exclude continental quality Africans and other black men.

So, certainly I'm not suggesting that any black woman get involved with a racist white man, and I obviously don't believe that *all* white men are racists.

However, keep in mind that my blog is mainly aimed at African American women of a particular demographic or to use a certain almost-taboo word in this country—class. Also keep in mind that my definition of "class" leans mostly on "values" not money. In terms of sheer numbers of men who a typical black woman from that class comes into contact with on a daily basis (through work, school, etc.), and who can relate to her and who she can relate to, white men are easily the *largest* pool of non-black and non-African American men in the U.S. to consider.

To use a "fishing" analogy, if I'm going to go fishing, I want to go where there are the greatest numbers of fish. That way, if I don't like the first few I catch, I can throw them back and get another one's that's more to my liking. There are numerous other non-white and non-African American men in this country, but their numbers pale in comparison to wm.

Also, many black women in the U.S. do not live in or near these usually urban areas where there are large numbers of these "other" men (Asians and Hispanics). Many black people seem to also forget that *some* Asians and Hispanics are intolerant of African Americans. Some among these other groups are racist in their views and many of those men desire a white-skinned woman, particularly for marriage.

> *I would never feel comfortable being in a relationship w/a white man, with a Tom.*

Well, I realize that an IR relationship with a white man—of any type—is not for every black woman and I've said that too. My blog is aimed at *only* those black women who are open and receptive to a relationship with the large number of white and other non-black men who find black women to be beautiful and desirable women as mates and who are open to commitment to a black woman.

> *And I certainly can't understand the obsession with mating solely with these men when there are a variety of other races to choose from if you're a black woman with no agenda other than love or looking to explore her relationship options.*

Obsession? LOL! Carria, it certainly sounds like you have an *"obsession"* with selectively reading my blogs. You really should go back and read *all* of my blogs and you will find that I've often used the phrase "white and other non-black men *and* other cultures of black men."

> *What makes them (white men) alone so special? Hopefully not the very "thing" that black men being maligned ad nauseum are accused of pursuing.*

Very selective reading. Again. You're the one who has connected wm to the notion of "special" in your statement above. Just keep that in mind because that reflects *your* thinking. You apparently have an issue with bw dating/marrying wm. The fact is there are a lot more wm in the U.S. and there are more of them in every category, which means there are more of them in the category of men who may be able to relate well to upwardly-mobile black women of all ages. Many African American men have certainly broadened their dating and marriage pool to include non-black women, but the vast majority of those other women are white women—due, I believe, to the sheer numbers of white women compared to other groups in this country.

> *It is peculiar to advocate black woman "broadening"(beyond black men) their dating scope...to just one other race of men.*

As I said, it's not *peculiar* when that one other race represents the vast majority of men in the country. Whites are 70% of the people in the country according to the last census. White men are simply "men." *You* (not I) have put them into a "special" category, an implicitly positive one, and you're now trying to twist my words to project that view onto me. I didn't say wm were "special." You did. Like I said, you really should go back and read all of my articles. It doesn't make you look intelligent to make accusations when you're clearly showing that you're being informed by your bias. You're also showing that you have an agenda. If you're not interested in white men as a relationship choice for black women, it's interesting that you're even reading my blog—at all.

Thanks for letting me know for sure that my blog is hitting home. When your type comes out of the woodwork, I know that somebody's getting scared that a lot of black women might just start taking my message to heart.

Fri Jan 26, 01:11:00 PM EST

Meli said...

Hi Carria! I have been a part of this blog for several months now and have greatly benefited from it. The purpose of the blog (to me) is to alert BW that we do have other options in dating/marrying. It does not promote a certain race of men over others, but the majority of women who post here (and sent their pics in) are married to or are dating White men. Also, the men who comment at times happen to be White men who are dating/married to black women.

Many of us have dated men from other countries and some were even married to men from other countries (black men)! Ethnicity and culture apply here also. So, if a man's skin is white, he could be

Scandinavian, Italian, Greek, German or French! Not to mention religious variations. I and the other women who post on the blog can only speak from the prism of our own experiences. I have never dated a Latin or Asian man...just never happened, but I am open to it. I have however dated white men and one Nigerian man, and black American men.

I date men who pursue me...and these days, they happen to be mostly white. At the end of the day, you are right—WM are no more "special" than any other man, but the man who chases and shows interest in you as a woman could become that *special* man. I say, promote who promotes you...LOL!

That is what comes across as strong and evident on the blog. It would be awesome to see more posts (as more women and men find out about this site) from men of all races who are in relationships with black women. Until then, I am just happy to see black women knowing that they too deserve love and have the *right* to define it as they choose, just like black men are doing.

I don't think that single black women who are open to broadening their horizons are turning quality men down based on race. American women, for the most part, have free will to date and marry whomever they choose and no blog is going to make them think that they only have one choice and this blog site does not do that. However, the black community does try to instill in us that we (BW) only have one choice (black men).

Meanwhile, other races of women are faring better because they allow themselves to be treated well by men, no matter what his race, and then go on to marry and reap the social and other benefits from such unions.

There also may be an assumption that most of the women on this blog site are American black women, but some here are from other countries in which they have always availed themselves of other men besides black men, and perhaps those men who fell for them were mostly white men.

I dare say that most of the men who are married, dating, formerly dated, or were formerly married to the women in Evia's sidebar, depict a great variety of "white" men.

Just my humble opinion.

Fri Jan 26, 01:52:00 PM EST

Ann said...

Meli, well said. Black women want a man to love them honestly and no one white man represents *all* white men, thank God. If you are a man of another race/ethnicity and you come into a black woman's life, come in right, or keep walking.

That is all that a black woman wants—a man who loves her, respects her mind and heart, and will do nothing to harm her in any way.

Fri Jan 26, 04:30:00 PM EST

Meli said...

Thanks Ann. We just want what any woman, heck, what any human being period wants out of life. You are so right: no one white man represents all white men. Tom certainly doesn't, but other than his cluelessness as to the monumental struggles of minorities namely blacks, and the climate of injustice which is ingrained in the fabric of our country, he is *far less* than the worst white guy I have seen/heard talking about racism and prejudice.

He wasn't the Bill O'Reilly or Rush Limbaugh type of white guy. You can't convince those guys that they benefit from white skin privilege at all. (LOL).

When it comes to black women opting to date other men, I am all for it. We as black women just don't have the room or right to turn any of us away from dating other men. I liken it to telling someone that she is only allowed certain benefits from life, the very basics, but nothing more. It is natural to desire a mate.

Evia made a good point about the numbers also. I never considered that part of it. There are more white men in the available pool of dating. They are also available in all age groups and they still tend to want to be married, even later in age, after a divorce and grown kids too.

Fri Jan 26, 05:55:00 PM EST

Ann said...

> There are more White men in the available pool of dating.

Yes, Meli, if I am correct, I think it is 7 white men to every 1 black woman in America.

> They are also available in all age groups and they still tend to want to be married even later in age, after a divorce and grown kids too.

Yes, you are correct. In fact, right now, I am corresponding with 2 men who are of my age range and they are very engaging to hold a conversation with, and they have many varied interests and seem like two men I would love to have as companions/mates in my life.

Fri Jan 26, 06:49:00 PM EST

Meli said...

That's awesome Ann! It is freeing and empowering to know that we have more control over our social lives than we have been led to believe.

Fri Jan 26, 08:39:00 PM EST

Carria said...

> I've certainly never said that marrying a white man would make his skin privileges or a racist mentality disappear. I've never advocated that black women get involved with racist white men or with any type of small-minded man of any race, for that matter. I have advocated black women broaden their dating and marriage pool to include all non-black men and also black men on numerous occasions throughout my blog. I had a wonderful marriage to a continental African man at one point, so I certainly wouldn't exclude continental Africans and other black men.

I respect the mission of your blog in its purpose, Evia, however in intent—from what I've read, albeit, not every single post but enough to get the gist of your message, I cannot help to perceive your work as a recruiting effort to boost the number of relationships that reflect your own, and, thereby, create a comfort (in numbers) that will someday extend beyond your (and those in like unions') doors. Again, from what I've read—and though you've stated otherwise—by all indications, the suggestion is that the potential for a healthful, loving relationship with marriage potential lies "mostly" with *one* specific race of men, which to me screams recruitment.

> So, obviously I'm not suggesting that any black woman get involved with a racist white man, BUT I don't believe that ALL white men are racists.

I was never asserting that you were making this sort of suggestion, nor do I know for sure if Tom is a racist or just clueless. I do know, however, that Tom's mentality abounds implicitly. I've heard too many stories from black women who were "surprised".. . they felt that way.

> However, keep in mind that my blog is aimed at African American women of a particular demographic or to use a certain almost-taboo word in this country—**class**. Keep in mind that my definition of "class" leans mostly on "values" not money. In terms of sheer numbers of men who a typical black woman from that class comes into contact with on a daily basis (through work, school, etc.) and who can relate to her and who she can relate to, white men are easily the largest pool of non-black and non-African American men to consider.
>
> To use a "fishing" analogy, if I'm going to go fishing, I want to go where there are the greatest number of fish. That way, if I don't like the first few I catch, I can throw them back and get another one that's more to my liking. There are numerous other non-white and non-African American men in this country, but their numbers pale in comparison to wm.

Evia, I can't address your above statements with any certainty because I've yet to see a study, that has/has not reached the conclusions to which you are speaking. However, based on personal interactions: family & folks within my closed-knit circle, I disagree.

Evia, I will address the remainder of your post at another time. I'm supposed to be enjoying the company of my adorable 2 year-old niece as I type. Look for my concluding responses on Monday.

Sun Jan 28, 06:20:00 PM EST

Evia said...

> *I cannot help to perceive your work as a recruiting effort to boost the number of relationships that reflect your own, and, thereby, create a comfort (in numbers) that will some day extend beyond your (and those in like unions') doors. Again, from what I've read - and though you've stated otherwise - by all indications the suggestion is that the potential for a healthful, loving relationship with marriage potential lies "mostly" with one specific race of men, which to me screams recruitment.*

Carria, you're making it sound as if I'm being underhanded about something. LOL! I'm very open with the message of my blog. However, you've gone from claiming I have an "obsession" to saying I'm "recruiting"?

I'm definitely encouraging and supporting African American women to pursue relationships with loving and loveable men, whatever their race or background. I'm unabashedly and unapologetically doing that.

Regarding white men? They simply are the largest group of available and marriageable men in this society for African American women *and* all other groups of women, by default, because wm represent the largest group of men numerically. Period.

There are non-African-American black men in this society. I married one of them (a continental African) once upon a time. I advocate that black women here include *all* interested men of quality in the global village in their dating and marriage pool, just like white, Asian, and Hispanic women are increasingly doing and at a much higher rate. I've never said there weren't any other men, but as I said, if I'm going fishing, I prefer to go to a pool that has a lot more fish rather than a lot less—given that time is a major factor for a woman if she wants to have children. When I wanted to re-marry, if I had been willing to invest another 2, 5, 10, or 15 years, I may have even found 'Mr. Right' African American man, but I may not have also. It's up to any woman how long she wants to invest searching.

I don't know exactly what you mean by "create a comfort." However, I would like for as many black women as possible to be in loving relationships with loveable men, just like me.

Lastly, I'm not responsible for your perceptions, or interpretations of anything I say.

Sun Jan 28, 09:37:00 PM EST
Meli said...

Hey Evia, I get the feeling that black women are constantly called upon to defend themselves for making choices—choices that for other women are a natural right. Especially for American women of any race, we have the right to date and marry whomever we choose. Why are BW constantly having to explain why we make ourselves available to other races of men? Our "dating out" numbers are still very small in comparison to that of other women *and* African American men.

Evia, I am happy for your relationship and all of the women on this site who have taken a chance on love with other races, and ethnicities of men. There is no "recruiting" of women on this site, to date white men! No recruiting whatsoever! I have benefited from knowing that just because we have witnessed a shift (for years) of BM dating and marrying other races (mainly WW), we don't have to sit on the sidelines and remain alone because other men are out there and interested.

Last night, I was in the grocery store and encountered 2 IR couples...BM with WW. I was not in the least annoyed because I refuse to limit myself to only black men.

Evia, it looks like if you want a measure of peace, cyber or otherwise, you had better start to have a narrow mind, do what others tell you to do, leave Darren and find *yo' self a good black brutha*...I don't care how long it takes, you need to give him as much time as he needs to decide that he wants to commit to you. And please stop offering encouragement to black women to get what they want out of life by not settling for mediocre men of any race!!! You must stop this mindless, reckless sharing of positive and uplifting information. LOL!!!

Mon Jan 29, 01:15:00 PM EST
Anonymous said...

I believe people see beauty first in those who look like them, whether they believe they themselves are beautiful or not. I don't mean "look like them" colorwise. I mean specific features, especially those of their own features they're most proud of. Beyond that it seems like a crapshoot.

In Alec Wek's case, it has nothing to do with her complexion and everything to do with her incredibly puffy face and beady eyes. And even the agency who first signed her didn't say she was mildly good-looking. I read when she first "came out" that was the regality of her presence/walk that won them.

And kudos to Halima. I won't be compelled to think she's beautiful either.

But I cannot stand it when white America promote a substandard "beauty" for black people just to pat themselves on the back.

Mon Jan 29, 01:48:00 PM EST

Evia said...

> *I get the feeling that black women are constantly called upon to defend themselves for making choices; choices that for other women are a natural right.*

Meli, it's also a natural right of black women and we shouldn't ever allow anyone to make us back away from our rights, or make us feel guilty for reaching out to get what's rightfully ours. Why would we engage in this type of self-limiting behavior? If we African American women don't deserve to be loved by a man and treated like we're loved and with all the bells and whistles, then no other woman deserves it. We merely have to claim this right because we already have it. Yet, we get hated on when we reach out to claim what's ours! Umph! And this hate comes so often from our very own black 'sistas' and 'bruthas!'

Furthermore, black women need to see clearly that anyone who tries to take this right from us does not really care about our happiness—at all. They're not thinking about what's in our best interests, no matter how they try to wrap it up in racial politics. No person should have to sacrifice his or her chance at love and happiness. No one should dare to ask another human being to do that because we only have one life that we know of.

One very interesting aspect of this is that I've *never* heard black men attack each other for getting into relationships with non-black women. When I scan black online forums and message boards, or even participate in real life discussions, the overwhelming majority of black men find a way to defend a black man's right to be with whichever type of woman. If anyone doubts that, just go and scan just about any cyber board. Black men have definitely got each others' "back" on that issue—if on no other one. Even the vast majority of black men who are all dressed up in Black Nationalism will still give another black man a pass when it comes to black men and relationships/love/sex with non-black women. Wouldn't it just be too grand if black women could do the same? If we don't support each other, no one else is going to do it.

Black women should all be supporting each others' right to be with whichever man is offering to love and hold a sista up high. I mean, don't black women ever get tired of losing out?

Mon Jan 29, 02:17:00 PM EST

Meli said...

Why is Alec Wek considered a "sub standard" beauty?

Mon Jan 29, 02:25:00 PM EST

Evia said...

Hello Anonymous, and thanks for your comments.

> *Nothing to do with her complexion and everything to do with her incredibly puffy face and beady eyes. And even the agency who first signed her didn't say she was mildly good-looking. I read when she first "came out" that was the regality of her presence/walk that won them.*
>
> *And kudos to Halima...I won't be compelled to think she's beautiful either.*
>
> *But I cannot stand it when white America promotes a substandard "beauty" for black people just to pat themselves on the back.*

Why does it seemingly offend you that Alec is seen as "beautiful" by *some* people in the world? We can each have our own opinions about Alec's beauty. I'm happy for her that some men in the world can see it. Once upon a time, no one saw *your* beauty either (if you are a black woman) or mine, but a few people have managed to grow beyond that conditioning. Beauty is a totally fabricated or constructed notion and is actually just a matter of opinion.

I ran across a fascinating article yesterday on how different groups of black people: Nigerians, Ethiopians, and African Americans view Alec. As you can imagine, *all* of the African Americans saw her as unattractive. I'll post the article in the sidebar in a day or so if I can find it again.

Mon Jan 29, 02:37:00 PM EST
Carria said...

> Well, I realize that IR relationships with a white man are not for every black woman and I've said that too. My blog is aimed at only those black women who are open and receptive to a relationship with the large number of white and other non-black men who find black women to be beautiful and desirable women.
>
> Obsession—LOL! It certainly sounds like you have an "obsession" with selectively reading my blogs.
>
> You really should go back and read all of my blogs and you will find that I've often used the phrase "white and other nonblack men.

Call it "selectively reading" on my part if you will (I prefer "intuitive" reading, personally), but my perception is based on the sum intent of your own words, numerous blog entries with a premise, links to formula type blogs espousing the exact predilection you back, along with photo representation promoting a relationship paradigm shift (for black woman) which not only supports the foundation argument but, again, mirrors your individual choice.

There are Latino men with numbers that continue to grow in every census too; Asian men, other non-white males who should merit consideration, yet your 'no unloved black woman left behind' mission has zoned in on white men as the most viable & redemptive relationship option. That's *certainly* not broadening the pool!

> Thanks for letting me know for sure that my blog is hitting home. LOL! When your type comes out of the woodwork, I know that somebody's getting scared that a lot of black women might just start taking my message to heart.

Those are telling sentiments. Your blog is littered with similar droppings. It's clearly you getting scared. Scared that there aren't enough of your type to validate your experience & have therefore resorted to recruiting for numbers from the same pool (not in every case, to be sure) of "settle" to which you once belonged; scared that the stats don't lie—white men marry white women more than seventy-percent of the time & when they are not doing so they are going for Asians & Hispanics; scared that white men, who, having infinite choices, won't even look at a sista once much less twice due to stereotypes that dog her race coupled with his own prejudice, so you crusade for "softening"/making more accessible black women who are open to tolerating those intolerances at the risk of never being happy or in a loving relationship or *gasp* marriageable. But I have the agenda. Right.

Mon Jan 29, 02:52:00 PM EST

Meli said...

You know, with all the money our community has, we could start our own modeling agencies, since we don't like who "the Man" is passing off on the world as the symbol of black beauty. But, we would end up with only near white models in it anyway because that is how much some blacks hate themselves...so, in essence, we can't be relied upon to be fair, and unbiased anyway. Why are we complaining about Alec Wek? We are so very brainwashed indeed!

As far as movies, when we are in charge, we can decide who stars in them. India has a booming motion picture industry (Bollywood) and spectrums of their own people appear in them. They are not waiting on Britain, or Hollywood to cast them or validate them!

We are mad at the wrong stuff. With our closed and narrowed views of beauty, what would a girl like Alec Wek do if she were looking for validation in the African American community? We have all kinds of "looks" and features in our communities. Thank goodness others see beauty in what others deem unattractive. I am happy that Alec is benefiting at least financially and she is able to build hospitals in her home country. She is helping her community—not tearing it down and insulting the looks of her fellow black sisters.

Mon Jan 29, 03:06:00 PM EST

Evia said...

Carria, you keep talking about my 'intent.' You do not know what my 'intent' is. You're merely "speculating" about what you think is my 'intent' and projecting your interpretations or opinions on my words. Intuition? People had *your* type of 'intuition' at the Salem Witch trials too and could just figure out who was a 'witch.' Ha! This is laughable because I'm saying outright what I want to say. I'm not being underhanded. Don't get it twisted!

Here's the thing: Smart women are casting in the ocean where there's the greatest probability of finding the most compatible and highest quality fish (males) because time is a major element for women especially if those women want to reproduce. Some women don't view skin shade, race, ethnicity, etc. as a biggie. I'm one of those women and I advocate that option—for best results. Lots of African American women should do the same. That's my message—pure and simple. The way I see it is that *all* interested men are potentially available. It just makes the most sense to me to cast the hook in the ocean where there are plenty of interested men of all types and anyone who bites should be scrutinized as for whether he meets the woman's criteria for a mate.

When I was dating, I never mingled with Asian men and the few Asian men I encountered never expressed interest in me. I didn't live in an area where there were middle class Hispanic men and didn't encounter many of them at work or school. Also, I wasn't about to get involved with any man who was not suitable or compatible with me in terms of my values.

Here's a very big difference between my philosophy and yours. I don't see black women as being less desirable to non-racist white or other men. I consider myself to be as desirable as any woman from any group to a progressive, non-racist, open-minded, man and I'm not interested in any other type of man.

> *There are Latino men— with numbers that continue to grow in every census too; Asian men; other non-white males who should merit consideration yet your no unloved black woman left behind mission has zoned in on white men as the most viable & redemptive relationship option. That's certainly not broadening the pool!*

Carria, you're mad as hell at all white men and you can't stand it that I and some other black women are not. *Are you even a woman? A black woman?*

Another thing is that a lot of those Latino and Asian men don't have love for black women, and you need to catch a clue about that. I'm not stopping any black woman from getting interested in any man!

You give me enormous power if you think I can prevent bw from dating or marrying that "growing" number of Hispanic and Asian men. My site is just one site on the internet. You are perfectly free to start your own blog with your own focus and 'zone' in on anyone or anything you please. Good Luck!

Mon Jan 29, 03:22:00 PM EST
Ann said...

> *Evia, it looks like if you want a measure of peace, cyber or otherwise, you had better start to have a narrow mind, do what others tell u to do, leave Darren and find yo' self a good black brutha...I don't care how long it takes, you need to give him as much time as he needs to decide that he wants to commit to you. And please stop offering encouragement to black women to get what they want out of life by not settling for mediocre men of any race!!! You must stop this mindless, reckless sharing of positive and uplifting information. LOL!*

HA! HA! HA! Meli, you have the wit to be a comedienne! LOL!

Mon Jan 29, 04:47:00 PM EST
Evia said...

> *We are mad at the wrong stuff. With our closed and narrowed views of beauty, what would a girl like Alec Wek do if she were looking for validation in the black American community (if she were black American); we have all kinds of "looks" and features in our communities. Thank goodness there are others who see beauty in what others deem unattractive. I am happy that Alec is benefiting at least financially and she is able to build hospitals in her home country. She is helping her community — not tearing it*

> down and insulting the looks of her fellow black sisters."

Exactly, Meli! If Alec Wek had grown up in the U.S., she would have lived a mangy dog's life! Most likely, folks in her family and community would have torn her self-esteem to shreds before she even went to school! She would have had no self-confidence and would have had a very negative view of herself in every way possible. I'm so happy that she didn't have to grow up in this country! Despite how African Americans are so sad about all of those terrible things happening to those po' Sudanese, she managed to come out of that hellhole thinking she's beautiful. Imagine that!

Still some of our own here are talking about her, slamming her! You're right—a black American modeling agency would have *never* hired her. As a matter of fact, she would have been diagnosed as *'certified delusional'* if she had ever tried to get a job as a model here.

Just look at all the black men and hateful black women who keep talking about how *'ugly'* Oprah is without makeup or how *'ugly'* Whoopi Goldberg is. Black folks get on my last nerve—always calling others (almost always another black person) "ugly"—trying to destroy the self esteem of others who look *just like them.*

I have to go back to what Darren said: Black folks need to "re-learn" how to see themselves as beautiful because the fact is that black self-esteem is demolished in black neighborhoods and in black social circles by other self-hating black people. Yet some of these same folks are mad as hell at 'de evil white man.' LOL! And when you call them out, they claim that the de evil white man made 'em do it! Whew!

Mon Jan 29, 05:11:00 PM EST
Anonymous said...

> African American women should all be supporting each others' RIGHT to be with whichever man is offering to love and hold a sista up high. I mean, don't black women ever get tired of losing out

Sadly, some never do. And those pitiful women feel *most* comfortable and at ease when other black women are in the same sorry lot that they're in. There are plenty of families where 3 generations or more of black women have lost out in so many ways. Losing out is comfortable, or rather familiar to them. And these women honestly believe their futures—when it comes to relationships/marriage—are truly out of their hands. It all has to do with "luck" or whether or not the Lord intends for them to be married or not. Truly delusional thinking. Behaviors and situations that are seen as clearly abnormal in non-black populations have become normalized in many African-American women's minds simply because they have not rewritten their life scripts.

Early in life, we all develop "life scripts" of the way we think our life is supposed to turn out. Then as we grow older and actually live our lives, we at some point discover that life has deviated from the script. Those who are happy and at peace in this world are those who can accept that a deviation has taken place and do what's necessary to improvise a new "life script". Those who can't, for whatever reason, run the risk of ending up like Miss Havisham in the Charles Dickens story Great Expectations. As a young woman, Miss Havisham was jilted by her fiancé' 20 minutes before her nine o'clock wedding. She lost her mind, and spent the rest of her life wandering around her house in a faded wedding dress, keeping a decaying feast on her table, surrounded by clocks stopped at twenty minutes to nine.

Basically, when we can't (or won't) rewrite our life scripts, we run the risk of living in the past instead of in the here and now. And in the here and now is where's it's at. There is absolutely *no* rational reason on earth why any attractive, intelligent, decent, black women in 2007 is *manless*—unless she wants to be.

Smart African American women (and black women of other nationalities) are already exercising their right to be with good men regardless of "race" whether so-called *sistas*, *brothas*, or anyone else likes it, or not.

And our numbers are growing.

Mon Jan 29, 05:40:00 PM EST

Meli said...

LOL...thanks Ann. I laughed at that after I finished typing it and thought, I probably should not press "send," but then that point needed to be driven home with biting, light sarcasm.

Carria, I figured that your posts would eventually turn ugly. Your comments that Evia's blog is "littered" with certain sentiments and that she is clearly getting "scared" about "her type" being not enough to validate...whatever!

If you don't want to date other men...then *don't*! What difference does it make to you what other women do? You seem like you are here to pick a fight or something. You won't change anyone's mind. There are women on this blog who are married to white men and have children by them. Are you throwing stones at those unions? I guess those women should have just said NO! They should have said no to being wives and mothers.

So what if most WM marry WW...black people are a minority in the U.S. (fewer in numbers—13%), so of course you won't see most WM married to BW, duh!! I was waiting on that scare tactic to be unleashed! LOL! Carria, you cannot change black men into a "one-race" seeing group, just like this blog cannot turn BW into a "one-race" seeing group. The message is that yes, we have other options!!

Lastly Carria, If you are married, you have no right suggesting that black women should not (mainly) date white men (since it appears that they are the ones you have a problem with). If you are single, you really don't have the right (my opinion).

If you want to wait or look for the perfect black "brutha," then wait! I can imagine that reading this blog must really get under your skin. If most of the women who post were married to Asians or Hispanics, you would complain that they are passing up white men! Personally, I don't "fool with" (southern term) folks who refuse to think outside the box, or have a lowly mentality of black women. That said, I don't see why you get your nerves all bundled up over this blog full of black women who are doing just the opposite of you!

Your point is taken. White men marry WW more than 70% and the situation for black women continues to be bleak, and, we can do nothing at all about it. And yadda-yadda-yadda—in your dreams!

Are you mad at white men for marrying Asians and Hispanics? That comment made by you is "telling." I'm shaking in my boots at the thought of those ever so truthful stats, because like you said, "the stats don't lie!" LOL! 70% Oh no!!

Now, if you will excuse me, I have to get ready for my date with a white man (our third). I guess I have to wear heels. My boots are ruined.

However, my apologies in advance if I have misrepresented anything that you have stated or if I misspelled your name, but I do not apologize for the sarcasm. LOL!

Mon Jan 29, 07:02:00 PM EST

Meli said...

I left out an element to my comment above. White women outnumber black women, so for any man esp. white, he has more white women to choose from, so you will see greater numbers of those unions. That's *obvious*, but that is not bad news for black women. The world is huge. This is only the U.S. I could be wrong here, but I would say that a disproportionate amount of black men date/marry out, especially considering our minority (numbers) status, and the numbers of BM in jails and the gay population amongst them further decrease the ones of them who are willing and able to marry. Bw who want to marry have to think about all of these factors.

Mon Jan 29, 07:26:00 PM EST

Ann said...

Meli. Wow. Ummm.....................enjoy your date.

Anonymous said...

'Offended' is the perfect word. It's not just Alec Wek. I'm offended when media hypes anyone as beautiful when I don't think they are, whether they be black or not, male or female. White media does this all the time—check the irony of your statement—with all kinds of people. If something or someone has features/structures that I don't like, then that person, that building, that floor plan, that car is not beautiful to me.

"Brainwashing" is an excuse to blame anything for our unwillingness to accept that what we may feel/believe may be unacceptable to others. Everyone should just accept that beauty is in the eye of the beholder, even if others think that eye is clouded with glaucoma. Individuals know their experiences. Individuals know what they know. Individuals think what they think. All we can do is ask, "Are you serious?" or say, "I cannot believe you think that," or something else to express our own opinions and maybe something that gives insight to where we're coming from.

So, again, if features aren't akin to mine (which I mostly love), then I have to step outside of myself to see someone as pretty. I value my features above all others, and see beauty more quickly in people who possess the same than in those who do not. And she, among others, does not.

That's probably where I'm losing it though...pretty vs. beautiful.

There are exclusively beautiful people in the world, more than exclusively pretty ones. Thank God for the beautiful ones, pretty or not. So Alec could be beautiful, but she'll never be pretty to me and I have never heard anyone say she was *pretty*—just "beautiful."

On another note: Someone please tell me how a black chick who is not light, has neither overwhelmingly Euro nor African features (good mix of what we were), has regular relaxed hair (sweeping over shoulders), not thin—attracts more white men than black? Sad to say, usually *married* white men—senior execs to guys in Publix with their wives coming around the corner.

Love the site. And the comments here are refreshing. Thank you so much. Good night to all around.

Mon Jan 29, 08:08:00 PM EST

Clarice said...

@Carria:

Clearly, your mind is made up which is fine. This blog is about exchanging idea, presenting different points of view and/or exchanging information among participants. Some women are curious, others are offended, still others are intrigued and curious to learn. Seeking knowledge is the key to power—personal, professional, and otherwise. Personal power is scary and owning that power is even scarier for some folks.

Folks that impart knowledge via sharing and discourse have throughout history—shaped and changed the world. Words have power beyond the speaker and that scares people. Thank you for your point of view. No one here is trying to do that. It is a shame that your fear will not allow room in your worldview for others to be and see who they choose to be.

Meli, you are so right. We should surrender our power and fish in a narrow pond and fail to live up to our potential (NOT!) Thanks for the humor!

The world is a great big place and there are many options to consider. Historically, BW have not availed themselves of options largely because they were unaware that there were options or discouraged from exploring them. I think this blog is a means to share information for the reader to use, or not.

Personally, I refuse to let others define me and my world, with so much to choose from and the countless number of people who died and suffered so that the right to choose was available. It is a crime not to be open to experience as much as possible with my fellow human beings.

Evia, this blog and the free exchange of ideas empower people to choose, or not to choose. Thanks so much!

Glossary

Abbreviations, Colloquialisms, & Vernacular Speech

Please refer below for the meanings of unfamiliar abbreviations and terms used in the essays and conversations.

- AA—African-American
- AA—Affirmative Action
- ABCs—acronym for the "Acting Black Crew"—a subculture of African-Americans who subscribe to a mentality and behavior code that runs counter to that of the majority *white* mainstream, i.e. rejecting good school performance, devaluing marriage, etc.
- Am—Asian man
- Anywhoo—vernacular for 'anyway'
- Aw—Asian woman
- Baby daddy—a man, usually promiscuous, who has children by a woman (sometimes several women) without financial, emotional, and/or legal commitment or contributions, and usually abandons the woman and child(ren).
- Baby mama—an unmarried woman who has a child(ren) by a man and sometimes several men without securing prior emotional, financial, and/or legal commitment or support
- B/c—because
- Bc—black community
- Bf—black female

- "BLACK"—a black person who goes to great lengths to demonstrate that they embrace black nationalists views
- Bm—black male/man
- Brotha/brotha(s)/brutha(s)—brother/brothers (usually refers to black men, particularly those in the African Diaspora
- BTW—By the way
- Bw—black woman
- CCBC—central committee of the black community—opinion shapers; those in a black residential area who influence others
- Chile—southern colloquialism for 'child'; often used as a term of familiarity or endearment among AAs
- Colorism—the belief that lighter/whiter people are more attractive/desirable than darker people
- Co-sign—agree
- DBR—damaged beyond repair—refers to a syndrome of undisciplined, irresponsible, destructive, intractable, and sometimes narcissistic, parasitic, violent/deadly behaviors that are usually directed against vulnerable, weaker others
- Diss/dissing—disrespect/disrespecting, insult
- Dog— promiscuous man
- Dunno—'don't know'
- Dyme—a woman considered to be extremely attractive
- Ghetto/ghetto behavior—a pattern of anti-mainstream and often uncouth behavior which includes but is not limited to excessive loudness, inconsiderateness to others, lack of self-discipline, gaudiness, lack of discretion, poor impulse control, disorganized, haphazard and chaotic lifestyle, etc. Poverty may sometimes be a factor in ghetto behavior, but it does not cause it. A ghetto was originally a low-income neighborhood where Jews lived, however in the latter

20th century in the United States, it became a densely populated urban area where hundreds of thousands of impoverished, disenfranchised American blacks who were victims of systemic racial discrimination often were forced to pay slumlords (99.9% white/Jews) high rents for dilapidated housing. Systemic racial discrimination and the resulting marginalizing and warehousing of millions of African-descended people in inferior housing produced hopelessness in many of them, who came to reject mainstream customs and values. A type of anti-mainstream behavior and lifestyle arose that is now known as "ghetto." In the U.S., many whites, Hispanics, and others also display "ghetto" behavior; however, the term is thought to be most closely associated with low income, urban American blacks.

- "Good" hair—hair with a loose curl or straight, i.e. European textured hair
- Gurl— girl (colloquial term designating affinity)
- Haf mercy!—expression of exasperation
- Ho—whore
- Hoochie—a promiscuous woman
- Hm—Hispanic man
- Hw—Hispanic woman
- IC/ICR—intercultural/intercultural relationship
- IMO, IMHO—In my opinion, in my honest opinion
- IR/IRR—interracial relationship
- Jezebel—persona and stereotype of the temptress/irresistible 'ever-ready' for sex black woman—a stereotype imposed on black females during slavery in the United States to excuse the sexual assaults on black girls and women by white men—for sexual plea-sure and to increase the number of slaves.

- Kinda—kind of
- Lawdy!—an expression of exasperation
- LHM or Lawd haf mercy!—an expression of exasperation
- LOL—laughing out loud, chuckling, mirth
- Mammy—persona and stereotype of a self-sacrificing, self-effacing black woman who neglects her own needs and makes the desires of others a priority; behavior imposed and expected of black women during slavery that is voluntarily or unwittingly still practiced by many AA women.
- 'Nappy' hair—hair with a very tight curl
- Old school—belief in and adherence to customs from an earlier era
- 'On'— arguing, argument, an altercation
- On point—correct, on target
- OMG—Oh My Gosh—an exclamation
- Oow—out of wedlock, not married
- Please!—expression of exasperation, annoyance
- POC—person of color
- PR—public relations
- QLL—quality, loving, and lovable
- Re—regarding
- Sahm—stay at home mom
- Sapphire—persona and stereotype of a loud-mouth 'tough-as-nails' black woman who uses verbal aggressiveness as a means of defense and/or to acquire power or to control others
- Shemale—a woman who thinks it's *normal* to perform the role of a man *and* a woman and willingly performs both roles.
- Sho nuff—sure enough
- Sista/sistah— sister (indicates an affinity with black woman)

- Sista Soldier—a sharp-tongued AA or similar black woman who considers it her prime responsibility to fight all racial slights or other forms of racial inequality, even when her black male peers express apathy and supply no help.
- Smh—shaking my head
- S-o or SO—significant other, steady romantic partner. For ex. a woman's S-o may be her boyfriend, her husband, or a man she dates steadily
- Sorta—sort of
- Stepping up—approaching to ask for a date or to interact romantically with
- trip/tripping/tripping out—extreme upset or verbally combative or aggressive behavior
- U.S.—United States
- VIP—Very Important Person
- Wm—white male/man
- Ww—white woman
- Y'all—you all or you (plural)

Acknowledgments

Thanks are also due to my "chief" blog researcher and the legion of volunteer blog contributors who devoted themselves to providing me with fresh links to articles, pictures, videos, and commentary to compel black women in the United States and those in similar situations to exercise their numerous options in all realms, to embrace the abundance in life, and "live well."

With deep appreciation of all who inspired and supported me in any way.

Author's Bio & Background of Book

Eve Sharon "Evia" Moore is an interracially-married essayist, interracial and intercultural relationship adviser, writer, podcaster, and producer of a growing series of books, newsletters, and podcasts on the subject of interracial and intercultural marriage. In 2007, Evia was interviewed extensively by the Associated Press over a period of weeks for an upcoming AP article on interracial marriage.

Her website, **blackfemaleinterracialmarriage.com,** was spotlighted in the subsequent Associated Press article that focused on the surge in black women entering interracial marriages. This popular niche website encourages women to embrace the abundance in life, which includes making the commonsense decision to take advantage of all of their dating and mating options by inviting quality, interested men of *all* races and cultures into their potential relationship pool. Evia points out that this often requires a "mental shift" for black women.

The site, that began in 2006, soon "morphed" into a popular Ezine that attracted millions of visits. Along with provocative essays and commentary, the site contains numerous photos of black woman-non-black man couples from all walks of life–from the rich and famous to the ordinary. "With my blog, I want to shine the light on interracial and intercultural marriage options for African American women. These are other choices that upwardly mobile African-American women have for love and marriage that are not often reflected in the black or white media. I wanted to urge these women to take advantage of the many possibilities for love and marriage outside their immediate environment, just as women of other races and ethnicities do."

Evia urges African-American women to "feel free to date and marry any suitable, compatible, loving, and lovable man of quality from any background in the global village. The 'quality' of the man and compatible values are the critical factors—not skin shade," she stresses, and "men of quality come in all skin shades and from all backgrounds. Lots of these guys would love to be given a chance to develop a loving, committed relationship with a compatible black woman."

Each book in the series contains a set of essays, plucked from hundreds of essays she has written, and accompanied by numerous comments from a wide cross-section of international readers. Evia describes herself as "dedicated" to spurring black women towards more fulfilling lives. She implores African-American women to engage in self-love and to promote and protect their interests 'first and foremost.'

Evia is the proud mother of two sons, and holds undergraduate and graduate degrees in comparative cultures (ethnology) and counseling. Aside from writing and consulting, she devotes herself to appreciating the arts, along with creating and selling her fiber art and jewelry designs. Evia travels widely and has lived abroad.

Black Women: Interracial and Intercultural Marriage BOOK 1—First and Foremost is the first book in the series that explores and documents black women's views on self-care and the intersection of race, culture, relationships, love, and marriage between African-American women and men from the global village, around the turn of the millennium.

www.ingramcontent.com/pod-product-compliance
Lightning Source LLC
Chambersburg PA
CBHW031348040426
42444CB00005B/223